This book is dedicated to my two daughters,
who are "my red sky at night"

by Caz Campbell

Introduction:

The term "Donkey on a Waffle" is from an urban phrase meaning to make something a priority or to get on with a task - "I'm all over it, like a donkey on a waffle". It's something my husband says and I love it because it conjures up an image of two things that make me smile.

Happiness, kindness and calmness are three crucial things most people prioritise. This book began with me writing bits of advice to my two girls who are 4 & 6 years old. I strive to teach them about the world, alongside them finding their own way. I started a book of notes and set up email accounts for them, and started sending things I wrote, pictures, articles, quotes - so collectively they'd be lessons in life for as and when they may need them. I found that there was so much advice, information and scientific research out there on how to be happy, calm, kind and live a better life that it was overwhelming, with a lot of overlap. I also knew some of the articles, papers and talks wouldn't be accessible in the future. I wanted to put it in layman's words, summarise it and condense it in one place. The book is a treasure trove of all the many tips, talks, quotes, therapies, books, groups and scientific articles that have inspired and helped me over 25 years. It is also a colourful journal, where you can write your own thoughts about each topic and come back to your notes. So it aims to be pleasurable and useful.

The aim is to get you thinking about various aspects of your life with regards to being happy, kind and calm. There are 52 topics focusing on areas of connection, awareness and fun. You can try a task per week for a year, use it as an A to Z guide to pick up & put down, or read it over a weekend then refer back when you want. Each topic has an explanation, along with scientific research, then mini tasks to try. Many are particularly meaningful since covid-19 hit, such as the importance of Touch, Environment, Motivation and Travel. I'm very aware that one size doesn't fit all so there are varied examples within the tasks. They are mostly simple, logical and free, but it's not telling you what you should or shouldn't do. Each reader will connect with the topics and tasks differently, so there is a space after each task for you to write any thoughts and ideas and "A, B, C, D" for you to make a personal quick reference:

A- Already doing this
B- Bookmark for later
C- Someone else's Cup of tea
D- Get on it like a Donkey on a Waffle!

Glossary:

The science in this book is for everyone so it's not too intense. Even though I'm a scientist, I'm not one for long complicated words making things harder than they need to be. The main things I mention that may need a slight explanation are these chemicals and parts of the brain:

Chemicals:

Oxytocin is released when carrying out an act of kindness, kissing, giving or receiving love, or feeling contentment, security or emotional warmth from someone. Oxytocin acts as an antioxidant and anti-inflammatory in the arteries, so is known as cardio-protective (protecting the heart). It plays roles in digestion, skin health and muscle maintenance. It also activates painkilling endorphins.

Serotonin is considered a natural mood stabilizer. It helps with sleeping, eating, and digesting. Serotonin also helps reduce depression, regulate anxiety, heal wounds, stimulate nausea and maintain bone health.

Dopamine is a feel good hormone associated with learning and rewarding seeking behaviour. It plays a major role in how we feel pleasure as well as our ability to think and plan. It helps us strive, focus, and find things interesting.

Endorphins are natural painkillers as they activate opioid receptors in the brain that help minimize discomfort. They can also bring about feelings of euphoria, general well-being, and improve sleep.

Cortisol is the main stress hormone. It works with other parts of the brain to control mood, motivation and fear. It plays an important role in a number of things, including managing how the body uses food, reducing inflammation, regulating blood pressure, controlling sleep cycles, boosting energy so the body can handle stress and restoring balance after stress.

Parts of the Brain:

The amygdala is responsible for emotions. It plays important roles in processing emotion and behaviour, including the fight, flight or freeze response.

The hippocampus is involved in the formation of new memories and is also associated with learning and emotions. It sorts and stores new memories and recalls old memories.

Topics A to Z:

Art	Mistakes
Be Present	Motivation
Boundaries	Move
Childhood	Music
Colour	Nature
Comfort Zone	Old School Ways
Community	Plan
Compliments	Play
Control	Positivity
Daydream	Relationships
Decision Making	Resilience
Declutter	Self-care
Emotions Part 1	Senses
Emotions Part 2	Sex
Environment	Slow down
Food	Social Media
Gratitude	Stuff
Habits & Goals	Touch
Healing	Travel
Identity	Uniqueness
Judgement	Values
Kindness	Visual
Learn	Warm Words of the World
Listen	Write
Massage	Your Tribe
Mindfulness	Zzzzzz

Art

Making and creating can make people feel relaxed, creative, calm and happy. Art can be an escape, a form of expression, a bit of stress relief or simply a bit of fun. Art can be drawing, colouring, painting, sculpting, crafting or anything else creative.

Art self-therapy is making art on your own in order to feel good. It's using art as a way of responding and coping with situations in your life, a therapeutic activity like talking with friends or going for a walk.

Art boosts your mental well-being and engages parts of the brain that are used much less these days as it reignites the connections between practical work and feeling good. An arty activity like sketching helps you notice important angles and shapes, patterns and shadowing. It makes your brain more alert and helps you absorb more detail. You don't have to be brilliant at artistic activities to enjoy them, the main point is to focus on the process. Your end product is for you and will be good enough. Creativity is less of a gift and more of a practice.

Art is a form of psychotherapy for a good reason, for mental and physical illnesses, for children and adults. Studies have shown that art therapy helps with eating disorders, dementia, psychosis, Alzheimer's, schizophrenia, trauma, anxiety, depression, cancer... the list goes on. In my eyes everyone can benefit from some version of therapy and art can be a fun, easy one. Art helps quiet the mind. Concentrating on colours, lines and shapes takes you away from noise - external noise and noise in your head.

A review of studies looking at children undergoing cancer treatment and the effects of art therapy found that drawing or other art forms can help in maximizing their quality of life and allows for a more tolerable lifestyle. It's a positive distraction, providing light relief from pain, tiredness and seriousness. It's fun, colourful and creative so brings the child temporarily back to actually being a child.

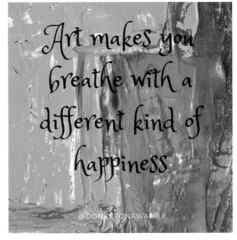

Art makes you breathe with a different kind of happiness

@DONKEYONAWAFFLE

Plus even a small sense of achievement ignites a boost. Another example of art psychotherapy is for people facing post-traumatic stress disorder (PTSD) and especially for those who can't or don't want to talk about their trauma. The mental process of creating art, bypasses the speech and language part of the brain and uses the same sensory areas of the brain that encode trauma. The part of the brain that registers a traumatic wound is the same part where healing occurs and art therapy is making that connection - it also lets people zone out and possibly release a block they may have.

Tasks to Try:

Look up some search terms that you're interested in, on social media or search engines. Whether it's drawing cartoons, re-inventing a piece of furniture, food related, a party theme, embellishing clothes or shoes, making something for the garden - and see if you fancy trying anything out. Remember it doesn't have to be amazing or perfect, start small - it's just for fun!

If you have the space, indoors or out, try 'big art'. Put a large piece of paper (leftover wallpaper / old sheet / newspaper) on the floor. Drip paint on it, make patterns, mix colours, try hand or foot prints, whatever feels good! Let yourself go with the playfulness and lack of responsibility, even if it feels odd to begin with.

If you have a garden wall, fence or driveway, try 'garden art'. Draw with coloured chalk or paint or even just water to make patterns. The rain will eventually wash chalk and most paints away so you can do it again. Or of course use outdoor paint to produce a permanent feature.

Your Notes:

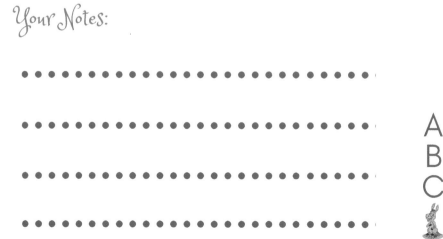

Be Present

The Mindfulness topic later in this book talks about being present without distraction, but there is also the idea of being present in what you're doing; appreciating and living life in the now. Children are brilliant at this, only thinking about right now without the worries of the world.

Adults are usually on a scale of being "in-time" or "through-time" people. Someone who is through-time plans a lot, looks and thinks ahead to future events, so can struggle to be really present. In-time people on the other hand can often get carried away living in the now, but struggle to plan. So they are often late, let people down or come across like they don't care, but it's simply because they're not thinking ahead to the next appointment or meet up. Just being aware of these traits can make you think and possibly understand another person who may have opposite tendencies to you.

Most of us are the same in that we seek out and remember negative news more than positive, because our human instincts are to problem solve so we look for problems! Neuropsychologist Rick Hanson, explains that our brains are like velcro for negative experiences and teflon for positive experiences. Positive and negative emotions use different memory systems in the brain. According to Hanson, positive emotions don't transfer as easily to long-term memory the way bad emotions do. Most of us don't stay with positive experiences long enough for them to be "encoded" into our brain's neural structure: "The longer the (brain cell) neurons fire, the more of them that fire, and the more intensely they fire, the more they're going to wire that inner strength - that happiness, gratitude, feeling confident, feeling successful, feeling loved and lovable." In other words, if you let a moment of happiness pass without being intentional about taking it in, it won't stay with you. So: stop in the moment of your bliss and acknowledge it.

There's a Buddhist technique for making the present count - spend 30 seconds consciously paying attention to the feelings you have.The feelings may increase and you'll encode the memory of the experience in more detail, so much so that when you look back and remember that moment, it will feel even longer. A friend told me to do this on my wedding day, as the day just zooms past in a whirlwind. She said at some point in the day when you're not talking to anyone, look all around you, take it all in, absorb it and you'll be able to look back and really feel that memory as you consciously took a mental video. I now tell my children to take mental pictures during their school day to tell me later and it helps them to remember the good things. Choose whichever wording works for you - bookmark it or take a mental picture or capture it in a bottle.

Tasks to Try:

This week, if you find yourself worrying about the future or dwelling on things in the past, try to be present. Be aware of yourself, how you're sitting or standing, think about your body parts, your surroundings and enjoy what you're doing today.

When you're in a moment of rest, me-time or enjoyment, take a mental picture or video. You could have a notebook of "those little moments". Or have a jar with a label of what year it is, then put little notes of happy moments into the jar - at the end of the year, empty the jar and go through them to stir up the happy moments you may have otherwise forgotten.

Your Notes:

• •

• •

• •

• •

A
B
C

Boundaries

It's a very common problem that people spend so much of their time doing things for others, that they become overwhelmed, stressed, fed up and frustrated. It's taught to us by parents and caregivers from a young age that we'll receive love, attention or approval if we do things for them. So most of us are people pleasers to an extent, but there needs to be a balance so we have the self-respect to live our lives on our own terms – in our personal and work life.

People can struggle to set boundaries, especially with people you may perceive to be more powerful than you or where you want people to like you and not upset them. It's a natural assumption to think if you set boundaries people will either push back or not like you, but how do you know this is true? And if it was true, is that relationship one you want to have? Boundaries are there for clarity and for all parties to feel safe and happy. They also affect your confidence, dignity, self-respect, emotions and energy levels.

We need to explore, decide and assert what's OK with us, what are needs are – what we'll do and tolerate, and what we won't, eg how much time we're willing to spend with someone or how much money we're willing to spend.

A lot of us find it really difficult to say no when people ask for favours or even invite us to social occasions. There's FOMO (Fear of Missing Out), as well as fear of letting someone down, but saying no can set a boundary and give you the space and time that you need that day. You're not missing out or letting someone down when you're caring for yourself, getting your life together, improving yourself or working towards your dreams and goals. Saying no sounds like a negative word but it can mean stepping back from negativity. Toxic relationships can put you off track emotionally, physically, mentally and financially. Setting boundaries protects yourself.

Not everyone is meant to be in your future. Some are just passing through to teach you lessons in life

@DONKEYONAWAFFLE

You may have been consistently let down by someone, but you justify their actions in one way or another. Or you may be putting in the majority of the effort and work into a relationship. It's OK to re-examine a relationship and start saying no. You may have mixed feelings about creating and maintaining your boundaries. You may feel guilt at not being the people-pleaser any more - especially if others are wanting you to meet their needs without question. You may feel uncomfortable asserting yourself but if you don't do it, it's unlikely anyone else will do it for you!

It's equally important to become aware of and to respect other people's boundaries too, and their right to have them - even if you don't agree with them, or they irritate or restrict you!

Tasks to Try:

Write a list of 20 things you would like to do. This can be simple things like going for a walk or bigger things like learning a new skill. But they should all be things that you would like to do from a position of positive choice and not from a sense of guilt, fear or duty.

This week, say no to something you don't want to do, whether it's staying late at work or a social event. Cancelling something or saying no may make the world of difference to you and your stressful or busy week, and may not make a big difference or any difference at all to anyone else.

If any issues or people drain your energy, step away if you can, even if just stepping back a touch like postponing an occasion. You can think about how you can change habits with someone, such as only meeting them in a group rather than 1 to 1.

Your Notes:

Childhood

Understanding more about children is obviously useful as a parent, but can also help you understand your own childhood, as well as adult behaviours. Most of what children need, adults need too.

The primary goals of children are to feel emotionally connected, to feel secure, to feel they belong, and to understand how they fit into social groups. They need to feel significant, to have a sense that: they are capable, they contribute to something and they make a difference.

Children also have a hard wired need for positive attention and positive power. If these needs aren't met, they usually behave in any way to get what they're missing, which results in negative behaviour. They then continue those behaviours that work for them, even if it's negative attention they're receiving.

If a child has loads of attention but is still having behaviour issues, it's likely to be a power struggle. They need and desire a sense of independence, autonomy and control over their own lives, which is age appropriate of course. If they don't get this, they're likely to do the opposite of what they're being asked and push buttons to get a power hit.

We're all born with free will. The decision of how to cooperate or listen lies with each of us. Most teachers and parents go to strategies that make children do something like timeout or 1, 2, 3. However, these methods often work against the child's need for power and they'll want to fight back in some way. When they do, we tend to punish, but this doesn't mean discipline.

Punishment mostly translates to blame, shame and pain. It can overpower a child with fear and they will shut down or lie to get out of it. Blame, pain and shame encourages children to lie, or take revenge as it breeds anger and

Where did we get the idea that in order to make kids do better, you have to make them feel worse?

@DONKEYONAWAFFLE

resentment. It also misses a learning opportunity and erodes trust as the person they love the most is doing this to them. There can still be consequences for negative behaviour though and these can be given in a gentle, respectful manner. They work best if the consequence is related to the behaviour, eg if a child refuses to brush their teeth, explain to them they can't eat any sweet things as they will rot their teeth. Or if a child won't wear a bike helmet, they can't go cycling as they could hurt themselves. These consequences are connected and can be explained without shouting, blaming or dominating a child. The child is then more likely to make the right decisions for themselves.

Rewards are another common method used by most schools and parents, including myself. But instead of building up self-esteem they can actually discourage and diminish a child's internal motivation. If children are rewarded for things they do, they get the message that they only work hard or help if there's something in it for them. There's been a lot of studies showing that children try harder or pick a more difficult task when they're doing it for themselves, i.e. not to please a parent or teacher to then get praise or rewards all the time. Being proud of themselves and having a sense they've contributed to something is far more beneficial than constantly trying to gain - and maintain - acknowledgement and approval from others, which brings about high pressure and stress.

Praise is very similar to rewards and this I find the most difficult to put into practice. Praise often means judgement, focusing on the person, and is rewarding a child with words eg "your painting is amazing" or "I think you're so clever / pretty". Encouragement, on the other hand is inspiring, focusing on the action, effort and improvement. I personally don't want my children to feel they need to please me or others for acceptance, or feel the pressure to be who I've described them as (eg clever, pretty). I want them to think for themselves and feel good about their own hard work and perseverance.

Our belief systems about ourselves can mean we gain a fixed or a growth mindset. Fixed can mean having a label (often imposed by others) or an expectation so it exerts pressure on someone who can feel out of control. Growth means someone is open to change, in control and has the internal motivation to develop.

A simple example is where a child says "I can't do this, I'm not clever / fast / good enough", this can be shifted to "I can't do this yet, I can learn, I can find a way to improve for myself".

Tasks to Try:

If you're a parent, be aware of how to make your child or children feel significant in the family. Be aware of the balance of power, control and attention. If you are or aren't a parent, look inside yourself on all of these matters – whether you adopt a growth or fixed mindset, whether you always look to others for praise and approval, whether you feel you belong.

Your Notes:

· ·

· ·

A

· ·

B

C

· ·

Colour

Seeing colour, especially your favourite ones, uplifts you. Colours have various subtle effects on people. When asked what their favourite colour is, my daughters would say "all the colours of the rainbow". When you see rainbow colours in the right order, it can evoke memories or feelings of being a child - playful, happy and innocent. Rainbows also symbolise togetherness and cooperation as well as positivity, creativity and joy. Here are what other colours can make us feel:

Red: Blood and fire! An intense colour that is packed with emotion ranging from passionate love to anger and aggression. Studies show that red can create physical effects such as increases in blood pressure, libido, respiratory rates, metabolism, enthusiasm, confidence and energy levels.

Orange: Symbolizes energy, vitality, cheer, excitement, adventure, warmth, and good health. Studies show that orange can increase hunger, energy, socialisation, mental activity, contentment and understanding.

Yellow: The colour of attention, caution, toxicity but also cowardice. On the other hand yellow can also have the power to de-stress and re-balance. If you imagine being outside under a mass of grey clouds then a breeze unveils a warm yellow sun, you may feel a wave of bright optimism.

Green: The colour of life, nature and energy. Green is associated with growth, harmony, freshness, safety, and environment, but weirdly also associated with money, ambition, greed and jealousy. Green is soothing, relaxing and helps alleviate anxiety, depression and nervousness. Green also brings with it a sense of hope, health, adventure, compassion and harmony.

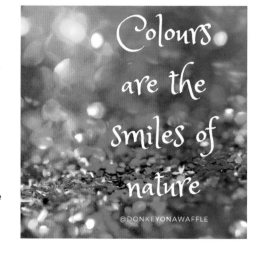

Teal: Psychologists say teal / turquoise portrays trustworthiness and sophistication. It has the calming effects of blue, which has been scientifically proven to lower heart rate, and the grounding natural qualities of green, which is thought to promote relaxation. It's also an intriguing colour as our brain wonders whether the shades we see are blue or green.

Blue: Sky and sea! Blue is associated with open spaces, freedom, imagination and sensitivity. It also represents meanings of depth, trust, wisdom and confidence. It can bring calm and coolness and helps with balance and self-expression.

Purple: The rare occurrence of purple in nature made it historically one of the most expensive colour dyes to create. Purple is therefore associated with royalty, luxury, power, and ambition. Purple has a variety of effects on the mind and body, including uplifting spirits, calming the mind and nerves, increasing nurturing tendencies and sensitivity, and encouraging imagination and creativity.

Pink: A 1918 trade publication stated that there was a general rule that pink was for boys as it was "stronger" and blue for girls as it was "delicate and dainty"! By the 1950s, this swapped over due to sailor suits and availability of fabric dyes. These days, either colour is for anyone thankfully! Pink is seen as powerful but scientifically proven to be calming.

Black: Darkness is important for sleep. Black has some negative connections but is also associated with importance, mystery, glamour, intelligence, sophistication and authority. It's a great colour where there is over-stimulation, with the aim of having a calming effect to either distract or eliminate noise.

White: White can brighten what is otherwise dark so can bring energy and light where needed. It can be seen to be pure, clean and mindful so can help get rid of stresses.

Beige: Despite seeming unadventurous, there are more words for beige every year - honey, cappuccino, biscuit, buff. It's a natural and neutral shade which translates into simplicity, serenity and comfort.

Grey: Grey has negative connections but is also thought of as safe and sensible. It can reduce overwhelming feelings of emotions as it is cool and calm.

Silver: the metallic refined, distinguished colour of riches, has cool properties like grey, but is more fun, lively, and playful. Silver is also associated with high-tech and future, as well as being ornate, sophisticated, and elegant.

Gold: The colour of the sun is of warmth, wealth, vitality and abundance. It can energise and uplift from dullness.

Tasks to Try:

Do something different with colour this week, whether it's wearing, noticing or eating. Be brave and have confidence in wearing colour in your clothes or accessories - bright socks, colourful jewellery, a bold piece of clothing, nail varnish etc.

Notice the colours around you, the deepness of nature, the brightness of paint or signs, the shadows, tones and hues.

Look at the colour of your food, notice the variety and freshness, and see how many colours you can get on your plate.

Your Notes:

A
B
C

Comfort Zone

Being in your comfort zone is where you feel calm and competent but it may not necessarily mean it's somewhere you love, like staying in a job you don't like. Because you know what you're doing, it's not stressful or scary. You may have had unpleasant experiences that means you avoid any similar environments, therefore creating a comfort zone. Having a crash at night may mean you avoid driving when it's dark. Having an idea rejected in the past means you may not voice your opinion in a meeting at work. Having been in an unhealthy relationship may mean you now struggle to trust or commit to a new one. Until you step out of your comfort zone and revisit something that you want, you won't know it's OK.

There's huge fear in breaking out of your comfort zone – fear of failure, the unknown, being hurt or judged. As described in the Mistakes topic, you can think of failure as a chance for feedback, to learn and improve. It's a good thing to minimise fear and stress, but a small amount of both can actually be beneficial. Eustress (good stress) influences us in a positive way by making life challenging, energizing and rewarding. Distress (bad stress) affects us negatively if not managed effectively. The relationship between stress and performance was explained by a stress response curve created by a practitioner called Nixon P. in 1979 (which was based on 'Yerkes Dodson Law'). There is an area they called the Comfort Zone which indicates the range of stress levels that we can manage alongside good performance levels. As stress begins to increase after that zone, performance levels also increase further – but, then we reach a fatigue point where our performance levels starts to decline. Ultimately, an excessive level of stress is known as distress which leads to exhaustion and burnout.

So, there needs to be a balance and awareness. Staying in a comfort zone can make you feel bored, unmotivated or disconnected. Edging or even leaping outside your comfort zone may lead to new experiences and emotions that you haven't had before or never imagined.

"Only those who dare to fail greatly can ever achieve greatly"

Robert F Kennedy

@DONKEYONAWAFFLE

Instead of concentrating on the fear or anxiety, it's best to try focus on what you may gain. You may learn something about yourself, someone else or something about life in general. You may feel in control and proud of yourself for a big or small achievement. You may grow in confidence and creativity. You may find a new passion, skill or asset. It also may prepare you to cope better with change in the future by pushing your boundaries and being vulnerable. Just like every other skill in life, you get better with practice. However, be aware of pushing yourself too far. Stepping out of your comfort zone forces you to grow as a person but if that force is too strong it can be damaging and can even stop you from trying other experiences in the future.

Tasks to Try:

Is there an area of your life where you'd like to challenge yourself? Where you'd like to try something new, improve at something or change something? Think of something in the past that you were scared to do but went for it – How did you feel before and after? What did you learn from it?

Most of the tasks in this book are about trying or doing something new or slightly different, if one is out your comfort zone, come back to this section.

Your Notes:

A
B
C

Community

Doing things with other people - connecting, socialising, learning new things and even reaching some sort of united goal - brings many benefits to your physical and mental health. Feeling part of a team gives a huge sense of well-being, belonging and often achievement. This is often through your job, as many people work in a team, or in sports but there are many other ways to be part of a team or community.

It's human nature to form groups, as we are social animals. Historically, we've always needed each other for survival purposes, as we each had different roles to contribute to the tribe - like making food, looking after children, sorting out the waste so preventing disease, building places to live, nursing the sick etc. Nowadays, most people live in communities where the same roles are still present. One person can't do all of these jobs alone. We look out for each other so it benefits ourselves and everyone else. As people get on with their role (and this may or may not be part of a team), meaningful interactions can be lost though, as every day is so busy and focused on the work.

People have a need to be seen and heard, to feel that they matter and are appreciated for their contribution. If you don't get this from your job or you don't normally work in a team, you may get it from social groups. Sharing a passion with other people lets us relate to others and can enhance that passion. These meaningful connections brings about a sense of community. E.g., a neighbourhood coming together to improve a communal area, joining a choir to learn specific singing parts and singing together - which could lead to performing at an event, or choosing an interest and seeking a local group so you can carry out your hobby / interest / passion with like-minded people.

We rise by lifting others

@DONKEYONAWAFFLE

Community

People connect directly to others within a local or physical community. People also connect through travel and technology, which has nothing to do with where you live and the options are limitless. Relationships and attachments between people who are far apart can sometimes be stronger than those living next to one another on the same street.

Sport connects people to each other and to places, (although it also creates disconnections). You may be a fan and have loyalties that emerge, saying "we" when talking about your team, e.g., in supporting a national team, or you may play sport for fitness or competitively. Sport can be a part of family life and traditional kinship networks that bring people together.

Looking throughout history, neighbours were said to provide the sought-after sense of solidarity, security and proximity associated with the word 'community'. But privacy is also key – looking at any street's infrastructure you see fences, hedges, walls, gates, doors, locks, curtains etc. that are designed to keep people apart rather than to bring them together. Despite this, in general, a neighbourhood is a place where people look out for each other. It's interesting to think about what role you play in your neighbourhood. When lockdown started due to covid-19, I knew a few neighbours to say hello to, but that was it. During lockdown, we took more time to talk to neighbours from a distance, clapped key workers on a Thursday evening from our driveways (but with a sense of togetherness) and baked cakes to deliver to each other's doors. Just these few gestures made such a difference to the sense of community from our point of view.

Creating connections is more important than getting attention

@DONKEYONAWAFFLE

Tasks to Try:

Join a group who share one of your interests or passions. This could be somewhere to go and do an activity together (charity work, music, sport) or could simply be an online group who share posts, ideas or Q and A's that you find interesting.

Volunteer to help you in your local community. Pick up some litter rather than walk by.

Start a book or walking club. Make a point of saying 'hello' to someone you don't know. Check-in with an elderly relative or vulnerable neighbour.

Your Notes:

· ·

· ·

A
B
C

· ·

· ·

Compliments

A few nice words can last a day, a week or even a lifetime for someone. It doesn't take much to give a compliment but people are often embarrassed to do so. But would you think a person who has complimented you, should be embarrassed?

A lot of people don't accept compliments easily, but one way to bypass any awkwardness or embarrassment from either side is passing on a compliment from a third party. E.g. "Jen told me how amazing your cooking is". It's nice for someone to know people are complimenting them when they're not there, plus it's harder to deflect or reject when you're just the messenger. If you're the one receiving a compliment, try your hardest to accept, believe and appreciate it. It's my first reaction to respond with a negative to whatever someone has said, which could be "it's really old / cheap / second hand" or "oh I don't feel it / think so". But saying thank you is kinder to yourself and to them. People feel good by giving compliments so let them - embrace the kindness that is offered to you.

Recognising others' good points and making them feel good, leads to your own happiness, as talked about in more detail in the Kindness topic. It is important to be truthful in your compliments though, as lying may backfire, even if it's with good intent. The recipient may find out you don't mean it and not trust what you say from then on. Or they may continue to cook you something awful because you complimented them once on it! There is an old saying, "If you can't say something nice, don't say anything at all".

Recognising yourself for all the good things you have achieved, however small, is also important. Self-esteem is defined as your reputation with yourself and is key to a healthy personality. The key to self-esteem is to write down the qualities you admire in yourself. Listing things you're grateful for is also brilliant, but this is specifically about giving praise or admiration.

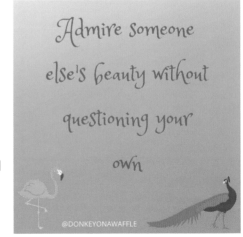

Admire someone else's beauty without questioning your own

@DONKEYONAWAFFLE

It's so natural and easy to compare yourself to others, but think about what you can do, what your body can do and what you have. Be kind to yourself and give yourself praise like you would to a close friend. Or look at it from a friend's point of view – what compliments would they say about you?

Tasks to Try:

Compliment three people every day for a week. You could even write down who it was, what the compliment was and how they reacted. If you're uncomfortable complimenting strangers, then think of birthday messages. If there's no one you know with birthdays this week, think and plan ahead to the next few coming up. Write extra words of love and positivity – why you like that person or how they have a positive impact on you or others. Heartfelt words that you've taken a bit more time to think about and write will be appreciated. Receiving a handwritten card in the post is always more personal but do whatever feels good to you.

Compliment yourself. Think of the compliments you give others, which of those also apply to you? Think of compliments you've been given in your life and absorb them – write them down and actually believe them! Give yourself three compliments a day for a week, or take on board ones that are given to you.

Your Notes:

Control

Control generally refers to how a person regulates themselves or wants to regulate their environment. There's a balance that most people would like to meet, of feeling in charge of their own lives as well as being relaxed. Our sense of control influences how we respond to events that happen in our lives and our motivation to take action. When we feel in control, we're more likely to take responsibility, avoid being influenced by others, work harder and feel happier. When we don't feel in control, we're more likely to blame others or circumstances, be stuck or unwilling to change and feel hopeless or powerless. Feeling in control is great, but we also want to be able to accept, cope and relax when that's not possible, e.g., when there are job losses or a pandemic occurs.

Stress mostly arises because of major change, uncertainty and lack of control. Now more than ever people are realising that uncertainty is a fact of life. It's so easy to assume and predict, but taking a step back and accepting a level of "I don't know" is something we need to do more often.

There are four positions to consider:

1) Unsafe uncertainty, which means danger, unclear, random, chaos,
2) Unsafe certainty, which is negativity, toxic, criticism,
3) Safe uncertainty, which means challenges, adaptations, flexibility, innovation
4) Safe certainty, which is repetition, comfort zone, complacency.

Which one would you prefer to be in? Most people would say 3. (Safe uncertainty) - as it's the most creative, explorative and helpful to our well-being and for improving ourselves.

When in uncertain situations, it can be useful to offer help to others who are also affected - a conversation can be enlightening and make you feel more grounded.

When you try to control everything you enjoy nothing

@DONKEYONAWAFFLE

Uncertainty and feeling out of control can be positive but you have to look at it in the right way. If you had total control and everything in front of you was planned, your life set in stone, you'd struggle to have motivation. We learn better when we perceive uncertainty, it allows us to dream big, to explore a wider picture and look for positives.

There is another downside to always being in control when it involves trying to control others. Attempting to control another person's behaviour is often caused by childhood feelings of powerlessness. But people don't want to be controlled by you any more than you want to be controlled by them. If we don't like the way in which someone treats us or acts around us, it's usually better to try to change our own feelings about their behaviour than trying to change them. Behaviours and habits are notoriously difficult to change in someone, even if they want to try. And if people are not interested in changing, it is almost impossible to make them.

Suffering and healing often gets met with a feeling of being out of control as well as a critical inner voice, negative emotions and obsessional thoughts of past memories. If self-blame creeps in, try to notice it as that and replace with a caring inner voice, one that you would use on your friend. Concentrate on what you can control and your attributes - write one down every day and keep reminding yourself of it throughout the day. Try mindfulness (see the Mindfulness topic) to focus on and appreciate the present rather than the past. Think of interests you used to have that you may want to return to or something new you fancy trying. You don't have to define your life by the damaging things that happen to you – you can write your own story. There is more about suffering and grief in the Healing topic.

Anything you can't
control in life,
is teaching you how
to let go

@DONKEYONAWAFFLE

Tasks to Try:

Think of the word acceptance. Accepting yourself, accepting others and accepting situations.

Write a list of things you'd like to change – which of these things do you think you could accept the way they are? Would you be able to accept what you cannot change or control?

There's also a task in the Emotions Part 2 topic regarding control and anxiety.

Your Notes:

· ·

· ·

· ·

· ·

A
B
C

Daydream

A definition of daydreaming is a series of pleasant thoughts about something you'd prefer to be doing or like to achieve in the future. As children, we're told not to daydream but research is showing that it actually has value and there are even workshops on daydreaming! As adults, instead of whacky and wonderful ideas, it often becomes more about thinking about our past experiences, imagining an event that might take place in the future, trying to understand what other people are thinking or making decisions. Virginia Woolf, in her novel "To The Lighthouse," describes this form of thinking in a character named Lily: "Certainly she was losing consciousness of outer things. And as she lost consciousness of outer things … her mind kept throwing up from its depths, scenes, and names, and sayings, and memories and ideas, like a fountain spurting"

In our unconscious mind, we find our most creative and inspired ideas. When we stop, rest, stare into space (some would say when we are bored), we can be apart from our busy lives temporarily and let our minds wonder. Thinking back to your favourite childhood fantasy story such as Alice in Wonderland, or imagining you're at a theme park or watching a pantomime - all the colours, crazy characters, funny things you may see, these things spark a bit of joy inside us. When we let ourselves just "be" instead of constantly doing, it can help improve empathy, problem solving and memory.

Daydreaming, much like night dreaming, is a time when the brain consolidates learning and may also help people to sort through problems and achieve success. fMRI (functional magnetic resonance imaging) scans show that brain areas associated with complex problem-solving become activated during daydreaming.

Daydreaming also makes us more creative and insightful, as we make

If you don't have a dream, how you gonna have a dream come true?

@DONKEYONAWAFFLE

associations between bits of information that we may have never considered before, so thinking up new ideas or solutions to problems may arise that we wouldn't have come to otherwise. This is where the phrase "let's sleep on it" comes from.

Studies also show that people who daydream about someone close to them experience significantly increased feelings of connection, love and belonging. However, thinking about unobtainable relationships - or faraway places or unrealistic situations may make you feel unhappy or less satisfied, so it's best to stick to positive thoughts. Similarly, timing is key as work or social situations could lead to awkward and embarrassing moments if you've been daydreaming!

Tasks to Try:

It may seem alien in our frantic, work and social or family orientated lives, but try daydreaming this week - while lying in bed or looking out the train or office window or while walking (obviously being mindful of people and traffic). Use your daydreams to help your mind, so think of dreamy things not nightmares!

Write or draw some of the things that pop into your head. People don't usually find your dreams interesting to hear about - unless they involve that person! I often tell people a weird dream I've had about them and it's funny for them to hear, and you're very likely to leave them wondering what it means about them!

Your Notes:

· ·

· ·

· ·

· ·

A
B
C

Decision Making

With information we receive, we may change our mind with a bit of difficulty – but changing our behaviour is even harder. We don't always do what's in our long term best interest, we are irrational and emotional in our decision making. But, we are irrational in a very predictive way! We care what people think, so we tend to make better decisions when we think or know others are watching or will be effected.

We also model our decision making and behaviour on others. Before 1989, seatbelts weren't compulsory for under 14s in the UK. The Batman and Robin series was really clever in being a great role model for children. Every time Batman and Robin got into the Batmobile, the first thing you saw them do was to put their seatbelts on. That programme may have saved thousands of lives.

To make some decisions, we think about chance of success but these are actually very difficult to predict or work out. If there were 100 lottery tickets for 100 people, people may buy one and have hope they may win. Imagine if out of those 100 tickets, one person had 99 of them. Would you buy the last one? It's a lot less likely even though your odds are still the same!

To make other decisions we work with shifting comparisons. We compare to other available options at that space in time. If you have a choice of three bottles of wine at different costs, you're likely to go for the middle cost as you hope it's nicer than the cheapest and it's cheaper than the nicest. But, if an even more expensive bottle is then added as a choice, you're now more likely to consider the 3rd most expensive bottle. Other external factors may influence a decision too, so things that aren't part of the choice but part of the context. So you may travel far to save £100 on a car stereo that is £200, but you may not make that effort to save £100 on a car that is £12,000. The £100 is the same in both scenarios, it's just the context that differs.

Good enough is almost always good enough

@DONKEYONAWAFFLE

You've probably heard of FOMO (Fear of Missing Out) but have you heard of FOBO - Fear Of a Better Option? We live in a world of overwhelming choice where most of the options are perfectly acceptable, but we waste time and energy over making decisions, we procrastinate. There are several causes of procrastination: time, perfectionism, resistance, indecisiveness, other people's expectations, feeling overwhelmed, fear of failure or success, or lack of focus, lack of purpose, lack of commitment or lack of confidence.

However, making a decision is a mini achievement, it puts your brain at rest as it reduces anxiety and solves problems. Decisions can set goals and help avoid negative impulses. If a certain decision seems too hard, then make a 'good enough' decision - even if temporarily - so you feel in control and to stop so much of the mental chatter about this one thing. Feeling in control reduces stress and making a decision also boosts pleasure in the dopamine system. Good enough is almost always good enough.

Tasks to Try:

This week, be more aware of when you're avoiding making decisions. Do that thing you've been meaning to do for months, or at least make steps towards it so you can plan when you will. It'll be such a relief. E.g., cleaning something awkward, writing a letter, filling out a form, book the dentist, get rid of the garden rubbish!

Your Notes:

Declutter

Having too much stuff around or a messy home or workplace can make you feel stuck, anxious, overwhelmed, claustrophobic and even resentful. But clutter is rarely recognised as a significant source of stress in our lives. However, having a declutter can be cleansing, making you feel freer, lighter and it also improves attention, focus and serenity. There has been an increased awareness for buying less and living more simply and sustainably. In Sweden they have a specific word "Lagom" meaning "just the right amount" which represents living in a simple balance. There's more about this in the Stuff and Environment topics.

Decluttering is basically a process of decisions, which is why it can feel like an effort to start and it's often a job that's put off. If you think of an object or space in your house you always walk passed and think "I must sort that cupboard / get rid of that... but never do. Even if it's a two second thought, it's a negative thought and all the times you walk past it adds up, sometimes for years! When you finally declutter that one thing, you're likely to have feelings of relief and clarity, and it also clears all those negative seconds when you walk past that place from then on.

Our relationship with stuff is complicated and it's easy to become 'consumed' with the act of consumption. For many items, it's memories and nostalgia, thinking that one day you'll use it, show it, look at it with your grandchildren or a friend. But, you may be keeping piles of books when, if you really wanted to have them again in the future you could buy them very cheaply second hand, and all the memories of the stories are still there. Having certain things can also be about feeling good or status, so looking good to others. However, when we give in to these pressures on having material things, it can mean we have less capacity to be interested in things and people that matter.

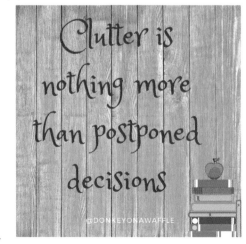

In a unique study conducted by researchers at UCLA's Center on Everyday Lives and Families (CELF), the relationship between 32 American, dual worker, middle-class families and the objects in their homes was examined between 2001 and 2004. It was called "the most unusually voyeuristic anthropology study ever conducted" by the New York Times. Researchers found that one of the most critical problems across households indicating enhanced stress was the high volume and poor management of physical possessions. Specifically, it was cluttered rooms that elevated levels of stress hormones in mothers, who used words like "mess," "not fun" and "very chaotic" to describe their homes. And that I can relate to!

Tasks to Try:

The biggest step is to just start, but you can start small by giving or throwing away a few things you don't need. Give yourself one cupboard or drawer or room to sort, and build up. If you haven't got time for a total declutter, just be aware of things around you as you go along. A general rule of thumb is to ask yourself whether you would miss or replace something if it broke or got lost. If the answer is no, give it to someone who would like it, to charity, to a school's jumble sale or throw it away.

If you have a block of what to save and what you can let go of – this is a good list to check first: old toiletries, nail varnish, magazines, CDs, DVDs, unplayed-with toys and games, clothes or bedding you've not used in a year, duplicate kitchen items or things you've not used for ages like spices or a pasta maker.

Your Notes:

Emotions Part 1

This is a huge topic so is in two parts. Most of this book focuses on calmness and happiness, which are deemed to be positive emotions. So these two sections discuss emotions generally and then what are deemed to be negative emotions.

Emotions and our attitudes towards them, have changed over time, many weren't named in the past and therefore not talked about or even known about. Nostalgia's definition has changed over time, it was once known as extreme homesickness. The Swiss physician Johannes Hofer coined the term in 1688. It was called a disease until the early 20th century. Before then they didn't know what it was as it hadn't been seen before or described so people even died from it.

Nostalgia and homesickness are now seen as different emotions. Homesickness has been more recognised since the 1980s, e.g., in children at boarding schools. It's generally thought of as unpleasant or distressing, but this can be very mild to extremely severe. Some people think nostalgia is toxic as it's longing for what was a better time, where our memories are warped, so this can be damaging. Others think it's a warm, fond feeling that comes about when you're reminiscing about the past. Studies show that experiencing nostalgia helps you relate your past experiences to your present life in order to make better sense and meaning. The result can boost mood and reduce stress. Nostalgia increases feelings of self-esteem, social connection to others and makes people feel loved, supported and valued. People naturally use nostalgia as a restorative way of coping with stress. And advertisers know how powerful it is as a marketing technique.

We either make ourselves miserable, or we make ourselves strong

@DONKEYONAWAFFLE

Children are usually brilliant at expressing their emotions, and naming quite a few of them. My 4 year old has it right in that when she is anxious she shows it, sits with it or sedates it. She can sedate unwanted feelings by colouring to feel calm. As adults we learn to mask our emotions from others as well as ourselves, we tend to suppress and distract.

The best thing we can do is be compassionate with ourselves and give unconditional permission to feel our feelings. When you feel safe enough to let your guard down, whether that's alone or with someone you trust - you can focus on a situation, fully experience the feelings and may then be able to better understand why it hurts and what you want to do about it. If you are feeling an emotion that you want to address, if you name it and admit it, it frees you up to do something about it. Describe a negative emotion in a word or two and it helps reduce that emotion. However, you don't want to define yourself as that emotion, so you want to notice the feeling. Saying "I feel stressed" is healthier and more manageable than saying "I am stressed".

Labelling emotions is one of the tools used by FBI hostage negotiators. Saying "it seems like you're angry", i.e. labelling a negative, diffuses that emotion. Saying "it looks like you're calm", i.e. labelling a positive, reinforces that emotion. This tactic helps de-escalate a situation because it acknowledges, appreciates and understands the other party's feelings.

We don't have to suppress, fight or get rid of emotions, but we need to cope with them, within our own control. We are the drivers of our emotions - and the authors of our own stories. Psychologist Susan David has described "emotional agility" as being adaptive, open-minded and compassionate. It's about facing up to your thoughts, feelings and behaviours - noticing them while being kind to yourself, remembering your core values and seeing the bigger picture. Then it's about making small changes to your mindset and behaviour, finding a balance between challenge and competence, so that you're neither complacent nor overwhelmed.

We all have emotional needs which we want to be fulfilled so we have a sense of self-esteem and self-worth. Everyone has different needs but just being aware of this list may mean you notice that one may be low: Attention, Power, Privacy, Control, Emotional Connection, Security, Belonging, Achievement, Fun, Intimacy, Purpose and Meaning.

Tasks to Try:

Think about each emotional need in the list below and ways in which they are and aren't being met. In which areas could you make some changes, who could support you in these changes?

Attention
Power
Privacy
Control
Emotional Connection
Security
Belonging
Achievement
Fun
Intimacy
Purpose
Meaning

Your Notes:

● ●

● ●

● ●

● ●

A
B
C

Emotions Part 2

It's important to know that we need all our emotions. They're all fine to have and are part of us, but they shouldn't define us. E.g., Pain is unpleasant but is considered valuable as it can benefit an injured person by preventing further harm or damage. However, what isn't helpful is when these feelings take over. As with most things in life, a balance is needed. And you have all the resources within yourself to form and maintain that balance.

ANGER

There are various reasons why people get angry: To correct someone else's behaviour, to demonstrate power or because someone feels powerless, to address personal conflict with someone or if someone experiences injustice. Everyone is different – some get physical whereas others internalise, some express themselves well whereas others write people off, some get revenge, some hold resentment for a long time.

Anger isn't always a bad thing. It can show passion, spark motivation and reveal better skills in certain situations. In a study, it was found when people were angry, they were found to have better analytical skills. Suppressing anger can be damaging, but it's also not acceptable to be aggressive to anyone. So it's vital to learn to deal with it in your own way.

Another interesting idea that gets you thinking is an 80-20 rule of your heightened emotions such as resentfulness, frustration or anger. If you get angry about something, usually 80% of that anger is derived from past problems that this current issue represents. Only about 20% reflects the actual current problem. Even knowing this can make you feel less angry. E.g., if you always felt ignored as a child or in a past

You will not be punished for your anger

You will be punished by your anger

- BUDDHA

@DONKEYONAWAFFLE

relationship, when you feel ignored in the present, you'll feel more upset than someone who hasn't felt this way in the past.

FEAR and ANXIETY

An evolutionary approach reminds us that negative as well as positive emotions have value. E.g., If our ancestors came across a bear in a forest, feeling fear was useful. Their amygdala would have produced a flight or fight response or they could kill or run. If that response wasn't there, they may have been eaten.

Anxiety feels like negative emotions but they can be useful. It shows you care about something and it can actually help motivate you.

However, you don't want anxiety or fear to be in control as they can be overwhelming and feel horrible, even debilitating. When learning to sing or in yoga, you're told to breathe from your belly - called diaphragmatic breathing - and have relaxed but tall posture. Breathing and posture are great ways to calm anxiety down too - relaxing your body, all your muscles, and letting your belly go out and in, without your shoulders lifting or chest rising.

Fear and anxiety can be heavily associated with control so it's good to gain clarity on what you can and can't control. An adaptation of Steven Covey's circle of influence and control is in the tasks to try.

Tasks to Try:

Draw a circle on a piece of paper and in this circle, write down things that you can control today or this week. They can be big or small but focus on things that are present to you at the moment. E.g., how often you listen to the news, how often you check your phone, whether you meet up with someone or not. Now draw a bigger circle around it and in this circle, write down things that you're worried about, and can't control. E.g., how someone behaves, what other people think of you, what's happening in the news. For each worry, tell yourself: 'by worrying about this, it won't help me...' You can then try and find the positive or reality in each worry. E.g., that situation has taught me..., the depressing news has made me grateful for..., if that person doesn't like me then they're not the type of friend I need.

A simple example to help with fear, anxiety and / or improve confidence is power posing. When you're by yourself, adopt the stance of Wonder Woman or Superman which can decrease your cortisol levels and increase your testosterone (which helps with confidence) levels, giving you a sense of power, control and confidence – away from anxiety and stress.

Reframing is useful when appropriate, e.g., if your train is delayed, instead of letting anger take over, see it as a chance to do something like call a friend or read.

Your Notes:

A
B
C

Environment

This is another huge subject so I've focused on the everyday, practical side in which we can do our bit and hopefully a bit more. How we each live can have a remarkable impact on the immediate world around us and of course scaling this up, how we all live, impacts our planet to an extent that's difficult to compute. There are so many websites, books and apps teaching us ways to learn and take action. The following are just some ideas - you may already do some, some may not suit you, but there's hopefully a good few you've not thought of that you can easily do to make a change:

Switch off chargers, games consoles, printers etc. at the wall. Unsubscribe from emails you always delete. Use less 'reply all'. Turn your phone or tablet off. As well as cluttering your headspace, use of these technologies use a surprising proportion of the world's electricity consumption. Only about 6% of all the data ever created is actually in use, that means that 94% is sitting in a huge 'cyber landfill'.

Take 5 minutes to read up on what can and can't be recycled. Getting it wrong may mean a whole load is rejected by the machines, but better than not trying at all. Plus it's a lot less time than you may spend hesitating when you're not sure over so many items. E.g., I didn't think glossy junk mail could be recycled but if it scrunches, it can be.

Stop junk mail so you don't have to do the scrunch test! Contact companies you keep getting unwanted post from. Opt out of receiving unaddressed items.

Drive smartly and you save money as well as the environment. Driving at 55-65mph has the most efficient fossil fuel consumption. Unload heavy items that don't need to be in your boot or roof rack. Keep your tyres at the recommended pressure. And note that heating doesn't use much fuel, but air con does. Even better - can you walk or cycle a journey instead?

Do your little bit of good where you are; it's those little bits put together that overwhelm the world

- DESMOND TUTU

@DONKEYONAWAFFLE

Go paperless - can any of your bills, statements or other post go online?

Travel less - With covid-19, local and worldwide travel was suddenly cut and people, especially in business learned they could adapt e.g., using video calls. People also started exploring nearby a lot more, rather than going abroad for holidays. Millions of people started working from home rather than commuting. Before booking a business flight, is it absolutely needed? And for holidays, can you go for longer and less often?

Heating - Putting on a jumper and turning the heating down by 2 degrees can make a lot of difference to your heating bill as well as the environment.

Water - Wasting water means we waste the energy it takes to treat and pump it to us (and for us to heat it at home). Could you have a shorter shower? Much to my husband's annoyance, I even shower with a bucket and use the water collected to flush toilets.

Food - Is there a lot of food waste in your house, can you reduce this waste by cooking and freezing meals with food that won't last much longer in the fridge? With takeaways - opt for no cutlery or sauces in sachets. If possible, bring your own containers.

Buy smartly E.g., washable kitchen sponges, refills, fabric or brown paper for wrapping presents, try not to select same or next day delivery.

Tasks to Try:

Pick 3-5 tips from the above list and commit to making a small change.

Your Notes:

• •

• •

• •

• •

A
B
C

Food

Most people know that a healthy diet can uplift your spirits and improve your mood. People who eat fruit and vegetables tend to live a healthier and happier life. Food is such a huge subject and advice changes all the time, with still many myths lurking about and being passed down by generations. So I've concentrated on a few interesting facts rather than what to eat or what to avoid, as that differs from person to person.

Our taste buds change throughout our lives, and it's thought that as adults, we learn to like things like coffee, beer and olives! Added to this, our perceived taste even changes depending on the situation - the time of the day, people around us or place we are at, which is where a restaurant with a clever layout, aroma and even wording on a menu, can tap into our senses.

Mealtimes or even snacking are often social as they're times of coming together with friends or family. Food is meant to be enjoyed and gives you sustenance and energy. A lot of mealtimes however, can be lost in watching TV, scrolling through social media, eating on the go as you're in a rush. When this happens, you don't taste or appreciate your food as much, if at all. Eating while our minds wander also means we eat more. When we eat mindfully, we enjoy and savour each bite consciously which brings comfort, joy and more awareness about what and how much we're eating so means higher satisfaction.

We all know to eat healthily, but sometimes the benefits can seem so far away it's easy to think "what's the point?" In a study of over 12,000 people, eating more fruit and vegetables was predictive of increased happiness, life satisfaction, and well-being, equal to the psychological gain of moving from unemployment to employment. These improvements occurred within 24 months, not decades later like some of us may assume.

The food we eat can either be the safest and most powerful form of medicine or the slowest form of poison

- DR ANN WIGMORE

@DONKEYONAWAFFLE

Food

Personally, I do not like the word 'diet' and I don't think people should use it around children. Children look up to and mimic their parents or other adults, so need to be hearing about people having a positive and healthy relationship with their bodies – aiming to be strong and fit is fine, not obsessed with trying to be perfect. Diets are well known not to work and more often end up being worse for you. This is because your body gets used to being restricted so it conserves fat. Forget the word diet and make a few tweaks if you need to, that make you feel good.

Things that help are having healthy snacks in your house rather than junk food and batch cooking healthy meals for when you're pressed for time. If you want to change your mindset around food but it feels overwhelming, the solution is to make small changes over a long period of time. E.g., instead of thinking from tomorrow you'll drink eight glasses of water a day, start by drinking a glass of water before each meal for a week. Lasting results usually come from consistent actions and subtle, meaningful shifts. There's more about habits in the Habits and Goals topic.

Drink more water!

Your hair,
your skin,
your body
and your mind
will thank you

@DONKEYONAWAFFLE

Tasks to Try:

This week, try to eat a few meals differently – mindfully, so appreciating the tastes, textures, heat, saltiness, sweetness etc. This may be eating outside or at a table instead of in front of the TV, or putting your phone out of reach and on silent. You may find you appreciate all your senses, notice your surroundings, taste and enjoy your food much more.

New Food – try new fruit or vegetables this week. Maybe something you've had but never cooked yourself. Something you've never heard of before – in a restaurant or look on different shelves in the supermarket / online. Try to add as much colour to your plate as possible!

Your Notes:

Gratitude

It may be easy to assume that happiness makes us grateful, but it's more the case that being grateful makes us happy. When you feel happiness, your central nervous system is affected. You are more peaceful, less reactive and less resistant. Gratitude is the most effective method to stimulate feelings of happiness. Feeling grateful activates the brain stem region that produces dopamine and increases serotonin production. Studies also show that higher levels of gratitude are associated with better sleep and lower levels of anxiety and depression.

An interesting part of gratitude is that it's the searching for something to feel grateful for, that boosts these systems. Just trying to think of something positive is enough as this is a form of emotional intelligence.

To live gratefully, all we need to do is appreciate the present moment as a gift. The gift within this gift is opportunity. To enjoy life, to learn, to listen, to teach, to help, to love. A method to embrace this way of life, of appreciating what life is offering you, is as simple as what children are told when crossing a road – stop... look... listen... go. It's the stopping that most of us don't do enough.

It's so easy to think "I'll be happy when..." But research shows that even if you achieve the "I'll be happy when..." goal, you're briefly happier but then return to how you were before. Switching this round can be liberating, by thinking what you are happy with now.

It's also important to be grateful to others by saying thank you to people, expressing your appreciation sincerely and without the expectation of anything in return. A study was carried out where people were asked to send a gratitude letter, explaining why that person had meaningfully affected their day / week / year. The senders consistently underestimated how grateful, touched and surprised the recipients were and overestimated how

awkward the recipients felt. Furthermore, the people receiving the note of thanks then viewed the senders as warm and capable. So writing a thank you note can boost someone else's well-being as well as your own and not be awkward at all! It's the little things in life that can make a big difference.

Tasks to Try:

Adopt a morning and evening ritual for a week. Each morning, write down 3-10 things you're grateful for. The more specific you can be in what you feel grateful for, the better e.g., I'm grateful for having an amazing partner, specifically for the way they make me laugh every day and we never go to sleep on an argument. Then each evening, write down 3-10 'wins'—awesome moments or little achievements in your life.

Look in the mirror every time you brush your teeth and think about something you like about yourself. Make it a habit to tell a partner or friend something you appreciate about them every day.

Surprise someone to show you appreciate them - with a picnic, a phone call, some flowers, a visit, a card in the post. Book something for someone's upcoming birthday or for no reason at all, to do something together instead of spending the same money on a material item.

Send a letter or email of thanks every day this week, surprising someone who's made a difference to you, impressed you, or gone above and beyond e.g., a hairdresser, teacher, shop assistant. It could make someone's week, month or year!

Your Notes:

A
B
C

Habits and Goals

Bad habits are formed when a trigger is made, which leads to a certain behaviour which ends in a 'reward'. So someone could be triggered by a feeling of loneliness or boredom which means they eat badly, drink too much or smoke which gives them a temporary good feeling. Behind every bad habit, there's a reason. People may eat or drink too much because they're stressed or lonely. If you think about what void you're filling, try to think of other ways to meet the need. There's nothing wrong with having that need, but if you're not happy with the way you're fulfilling the need, you could look at alternatives.

When seeking to attain something in our lives, it's better to invest our time in forming positive habits to reach a goal. Finding what resonates with you and your energy systems is important as these are things that you're more likely to sustain. It's also easier to form a good habit if you don't aim too high or think too vague. Having short-term goals or being micro-ambitious is fine and actually more likely you'll reach them.

My favourite tip is to think about who you want to be, so you're striving to be the best version of yourself, and then what you want to do or not do. It's a slight tweak to the way you think, but an inspiring difference.

People are very different in how they form or break habits, what works for me may not work for you. Some ways that make it easier to form or break a habit are as follows:-

1) Monitoring: so if you write down your progress or quantify your goals, this may help keep you motivated.

2) Pairing: which is joining the new habit with something you already do, e.g., telling yourself once you've tidied your clothes in your room, then you can get comfy in your pjs, or if you're trying

Remember when you wanted what you currently have?

@DONKEYONAWAFFLE

to drink more water, drinking a full glass before doing your teeth.

3) Treats: which doesn't have to mean unhealthy, but something you love that you can hold back and treat yourself once you've reached a goal of some sort.

4) Triggers: being curiously aware about a trigger that leads to a habit and feeling joy at letting it go - e.g., mindful smoking may make someone realise it tastes awful, or being very aware of wanting a load of chocolate and feeling great that you've resisted.

5) Commitment device: for some people having a 'commitment device' helps to stop procrastinating and start a habit. This is something you put in place in the present to lock you in to a certain behaviour in the future. This can be a specific method that works for you like: getting rid of your credit cards to avoid mindless spending, leaving your laptop at work so you can't keep working at home, buying unhealthy food in small amounts, rather than in bulk. A downside to commitment devices is that you may feel like you have no self-control, then when you come up against something that you don't have one for, you may feel powerless. Self-discipline or willpower is like a muscle, however, if you exercise it, it gets stronger.

Your actions are in your control, but outcomes are not always in your control. So it's best to "Invest in the process not the outcome"; Instead of focusing on the end result you want, focus on your present actions - even enjoy them!

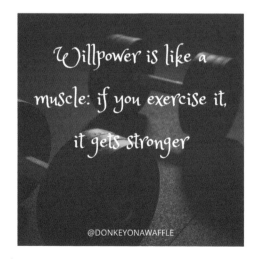
Willpower is like a muscle: if you exercise it, it gets stronger

@DONKEYONAWAFFLE

Tasks to Try:

If you want to make some sort of change, you can write your own story, think in detail what that story would be. It helps to visualise it and write or draw what you want. If it's yourself, where are you, how are you sitting or standing, what does your face look like, what are you wearing, what scents can you smell, what can you feel – physically and emotionally.

The Values topic also has a task for values and goals that's easier done together.

Your Notes:

· ·

· ·

· ·

· ·

A
B
C

Healing

Healing and grief can be about a loss of a loved one, a job or a relationship amongst other things. You may feel something has gone from your life and it's usually out of your control. Healing is a complicated process and unique to each person. It's something that every one of us will experience and it doesn't stop - it comes and goes, gets easier to manage but it can stay with us for a long time, sometimes forever.

There are known to be around seven stages of grief, but these aren't linear stages and time spent in each may vary greatly. They don't have to, but they generally go in this order:-

Shock: feelings of disbelief, leaving the grieving person feeling numb.

Denial: convincing themselves or others that the event hasn't happened or isn't permanent.

Guilt: feelings of pain and regret. A person may think they could have done something to prevent or help or stop an event from happening. Or they may feel regret from not being able to make peace with someone who has died.

Anger: feelings of frustration and wanting to blame others for the loss. It's totally normal to feel angry but to prevent the risk of damaging personal and/or professional relationships, it's important to learn to release emotions in a healthy way.

In your darkest of days, there's always a glimmer of hope... if you look hard enough

@DONKEYONAWAFFLE

Bargaining: trying to prevent permanent loss by 'making a deal' with someone else - whether it's a boss, partner or a higher power.

Depression: feelings of heaviness and loneliness - physical, emotional and behavioural changes such as sleeping

and eating patterns, headaches, crying, withdrawing. This is often the stage when
emotions may seem most raw.

Reconstruction: realising the effect that grief is having on their life and beginning to look for ways to cope and gain control. Trying new things to help improve their mood and emotional outlook.

Acceptance: acknowledging a loss while thinking about and planning for the future. Finding meaning, so it's possible to find hope again. It's rare to be at peace with a loss but regaining control of their life by acceptance is achievable.

Grief in a child is on another level. Each child is so different but they usually take words literally when young. It's so important to explain things clearly. It's the adults' job to start a conversation with a child, like asking "Is there anything you want to know about...?" "What do you understand about...?" Sometimes words aren't needed, but showing them you're there is important. If they can't talk about the loss, you can try to find what they find joy in. They may not know how they feel but can use toys, art, sand, photos, poems, prayers and more to illustrate their feelings. Expressing their emotions and allowing them to feel sad is so important. It's also OK to not want to talk about it, but they need to be told that they can when they want to.

If a child has loss when very young, they may lose part of their innocence, i.e. the fantasy that their parents will live forever. It's a harsh reality to learn rather than living in a world of fairy tale dreams.

Children need to know the truth as they will try to find meaning, otherwise it may be denying them the chance to grieve. They may blame themselves, feel guilt, shame or fear. Living with loss may affect their relationship with themselves and their belief systems. At around 8 years old, children start to think about death and need to feel safe. Explaining to a child that thoughts aren't dangerous can help.

Animals and nature are amazing sources of healing. They're both talked about in the Nature and Touch topics. But specific to healing, pets aid people to cope with grief as they are calming and non-judgemental. They provide company and give the owner a purpose.

Tasks to Try:

If you know someone who is grieving, don't be afraid to ask them about it – they'll either be thinking about it anyway, or they may need to talk or cry about it. Everyone is different but most people will appreciate being asked, even if they don't want to talk about it, better that than people avoiding them.

Think about what you may find helpful when you may suffer a loss in the future. Whether it's who you may talk to, how you'd take care of yourself, what professional help there is local to you? Thinking about these things now if you're in a non-grieving state will help later if something does happen.

One idea to help when you are grieving from a death is to carry out some kind of memorial or ritual like scattering ashes, or write a letter to the deceased. Another idea is to start a project where you're thinking about the person in a positive way. This can be something that the person you've lost would've cared about, like a charity. Or, something that reminds you of the happy memories of that person such as putting together a video clip montage of them.

Your Notes:

A
B
C

Identity

How you identify can be related to your body, your mind, where you live, what you do and who is in your life. Identities can be simple or complex, deemed as positive or negative, but there's usually a connection to other people, places and the ongoing activities of everyday life that make up society. Some identities are fixed or are very difficult to alter, whereas others are transient, changing throughout someone's life.

When we meet someone for the first time, a conversation often starts with the question 'where are you from?', as if the answer will reveal something about the type of person they might be. This comes from the assumption that identity is somehow connected to the place where people live or their place of origin. When we meet others from places with which we also have some association, this can help to break the ice and create a sense of connection. This suggests that people living within one place share a collective identity or a sense of common belonging.

Typical forms we fill out for identity purposes usually have categories of sex, age, nationality, race and ethnicity. Each of these may be a personal identity but they're also likely to connect us socially to others in that same category e.g., people of a similar age being in the same educational year, or people of the same ethnicity sharing the same social club. Disability is another category that appears on forms and makes us consider bodies as part of our identity. As well as sex and age, the ability of our body connects and disconnects personal and social worlds. Sport is an area of social life where our bodies and our abilities are really important. Your body might determine whether you win or lose, or even if you can take part at all.

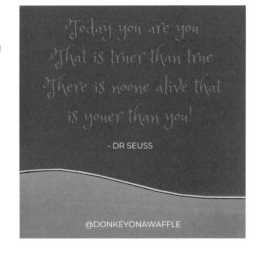

Today you are you
That is truer than true
There is noone alive that
is youer than you!

- DR SEUSS

@DONKEYONAWAFFLE

Many people feel that they have a unique personal identity, i.e. who they are, which is separate from their social identities given by situations, relationships and groups. However, these social identities can have a huge effect on our personal identity e.g., being part of a sports team gives someone confidence or someone's job makes them constantly embarrassed. Some of people's most personal identities, like gender, can also be social identities and this can vary from one society to another. Human beings are social animals, shaped by society through their life experiences, often in ways we're not even aware of.

Psychologists use the term 'label' to refer to a negatively valued identity which, once given, sticks to a person and is difficult to escape: e.g., 'labelling' someone as selfish or lazy is certain to cause that person hurt as well as encourage them to fill that role. A family who talks about their child as being "the naughty one" may cause that child to feel that's their identity. Your family will have a huge influence on your identity, as people grow up thinking their environment is the norm.

There are also many examples of a negative identity given to one group of people by another and this usually comes from unfair judgement, which leads on nicely to the next topic!

Tasks to Try:

Write down 10 things expressing your identity – how you would describe yourself to another person. This can be physical aspects, personality traits, what you do for work or play, what you love etc. Next, imagine you're a refugee, how many of the things on your list would remain the same? The idea is to help to clarify and identify your core features and parts of yourself that stay with you despite external circumstances or environmental influences. These are the parts of you that you can be sure of and embrace during uncertain times.

Your Notes:

· ·

· ·

A
B
C

· ·

· ·

Judgement

Most peoples' number one fear is rejection, and as a result we end up doing things to try to impress others instead of ourselves. We need to learn to be comfortable being ourselves instead of trying to be someone we're not. It's difficult not to be affected by what other people think of us but our self-worth should never come from someone else. Plus, most of the time you don't know what people think, and you're probably assuming wrongly. At the same time we need to be aware of others around us who will also fear being judged, and we should make a conscious effort not to judge too harshly or quickly. Judgements aren't all negative, of course. Many are positive, correct and a good thing. Some can be a positive judgement but not true, which can lead to trusting someone you shouldn't.

Psychologists have discovered that people make an assumption within 7 seconds of hearing a stranger's voice or meeting someone, and some research even says we decide whether a person is trustworthy in a tenth of a second. That first impression whether it's right or wrong, is difficult to undo so the future of a relationship is often formed from the first few seconds. We are quick to judge others on appearance, smile, handshake, body language and behaviour like being on time or mannerisms. When it comes to appearance it's important to note that it has been shown many times that sense of humour, confidence, passion, honesty, intelligence and compassion are all far more attractive than looks.

We don't need to have an opinion on every tiny thing in life. It's mostly better if we don't, because then we can be more open and receptive to new ideas and perspectives. Every person that you meet will know things that you don't, have experiences you haven't had and view the world differently to you. And this is amazing! Differences are something to celebrate and it makes every situation and person an opportunity to learn.

Don't judge me by the chapter you walked in on

@DONKEYONAWAFFLE

Many people think that they can mould their friend, child or partner into the erson they think they should be. Accepting other people for who they are is uch easier when you understand that the only person you can actually change yourself. And changing yourself is a difficult one as you have to ask who are ou changing for? I'm all for making improvements and learning but we also have o be kind to ourselves and not judge ourselves too harshly. Creativity dies in the ace of judgement and we can be our own worst critics. Children are gloriously reative due to giving their brains time to explore without judgement.

veryone has something that they feel sensitive or vulnerable about. No one likes o be judged so it's a good thing to remind ourselves how we felt when other eople judged our choices or passions. However, while it is important to accept eople as they are, it's just as important to know when to say no or enough is nough. It's easy to make excuses for toxic behaviour as it being "just how that erson is". But that doesn't allow you to be victimized, bullied, or harmed by em in any way. Healthy boundaries are a critical part of any relationship and ere's more detail on this in the Boundaries topic.

Tasks to Try:

iis week, try to notice when you judge too quickly, notice when you assume ither than have the facts, notice when you can go into a situation with no xpectations but with a totally open mind. Expect the unexpected! Ask uestions, explore differences.

eople are going to judge and you can't control that. What you can control is our reaction. Ask yourself who you're trying to please, and this is hopefully ourself and your loved ones, not those who judge you unkindly.

Your Notes:

A
B
C

Kindness

Kindness is one of the three major points of this book so is mentioned throughout in many topics. The Oxford English Dictionary defines kindness as "the quality of being friendly, generous, and considerate." When we focus our energy on the needs of other people, we increase our ability to connect with them. This builds empathy, stronger bonds and friendship. Carrying out acts of kindness can make others' lives better as well as your own life more enjoyable. Kindness is a source of pleasure and this feeling of elevation causes kindness to be contagious. So one good deed can create a domino effect.

Most people would think that the opposite of stress is calm and relaxed, but they are the absence of stress. Kindness is in fact the opposite of stress. Physiologically and behaviourally, research shows that as one increases, the other decreases. Stress produces the hormones cortisol and adrenalin, which increase blood pressure, suppress the immune system, tense the nervous system and trigger depression. Whereas kindness produces oxytocin which decreases blood pressure, lifts the immune system, relaxes the nervous system and reduces the risk of depression.

Studies looking at volunteers, show that on days with more acts of kindness, there were lower stress levels and negative emotions. Even when stressful events occurred, any negative emotional impact was lessened if acts of kindness were high. This doesn't mean that stressful events don't happen when we're kind, but our resilience to them is higher.

Kindness elevates the immune system. A study where volunteers watched Mother Theresa carrying out humanitarian acts on the streets of Calcutta, showed that s-IgA levels (a component of the immune system) had significantly increased after watching the film. So even watching kindness gives us feelings that promote the immune system,

Spread love everywhere you go. Let no one ever come to you without leaving happier

- MOTHER TERESA

@DONKEYONAWAFFLE

whereas feelings of stress can suppress it. Another factor is ageing - as we know stress accelerates ageing - this damage is caused by 'free radicals'. High levels of oxytocin (produced by kindness) on the other hand keep free radicals down so is a natural way to feel young!

Results of surveys from 200,000 people from around the world showed that a third donated money in the last month. People who gave money to charity were happier than people who didn't, even after taking into account their financial situation. Giving money to charity made as much difference to happiness as having twice as much income. Increasing happiness by giving, works much better when there's a connection - i.e. if you can envision how your money is helping. Giving isn't a moral obligation, it is a source of pleasure. This is also demonstrated in a study where people were given £100 - the people who spent the money on others were happier than those who spent the money on themselves.

Interestingly, the oldest recorded fundraising appeal was written by St. Paul around A.D. 55. Most of its words described the benefits of giving.

It's not all about donating money though. Almost half of UK adults say that their busy lives stop them from connecting with other people. We can all play a part to tackle loneliness. And it's incredibly simple. The slogan 'Let's Talk More' suggests the next time you're on the bus, at the shops or out and about, look for an opportunity to make a connection. Research shows even small moments of connection can improve someone's well-being and help tackle loneliness. Small moments can make a big difference. A smile and a hello can lift someone's day.

In a world where you can be anything, be kind

@DONKEYONAWAFFLE

Tasks to Try:

Help a stranger this week, e.g., ask a mum if she needs help with her buggy. Pick something up that someone's dropped. Let people into a traffic queue while driving. Let someone with only a few items ahead of you in a shop queue. Think of others' needs, if you can help someone, why wouldn't you?

If you have a conflict with someone, have a chat in a constructive manner and with kindness. You will be surprised how even most difficult conversations can go better if you approach it compassionately.

There are other Kindness tasks in the Gratitude topic.

Your Notes:

• •

• •

• •

• •

A
B
C

Learn

"Life is best filled by learning as much as you can about as much as you can" - Tim Minchin.

Being in a state of inspiration increases your energy and happiness levels. It is different for every person so a subject that may inspire me may not inspire you, but hopefully you're finding a good few topics in this book to inspire you to learn more. Learning can have negative connotations from your days at school but if you shift this to being a privilege rather than a chore, then there is no end to what you may find.

Learning helps to broaden horizons and encourage self-development. It increases the density of white matter in your brain and stimulates neurons in the brain, which forms more neural pathways and allows electrical impulses to travel faster across them. These two processes help improve performance which you can then apply to other areas or problems. So the more you learn, the better you get at learning! Plus it can help prevent dementia.

We usually think of recharging as relaxation, but sometimes the best way to recharge is to do something that distracts you. Learning something new, without the pressure of it being correlated to your job, refreshes your mind and helps you see a different perspective to things.

Reading is a great gift and can be an amazing source of happiness, whether you're reading to learn or to escape. If you don't often read, get some recommendations from friends - be specific about the subject or style you're looking for. Many people feel they don't have time or a quiet enough place to read. This is where podcasts or audio books can be amazing. Any topic you're interested in, you'll be able to find something to listen to, so when you're cooking, travelling to work, driving etc., you can be learning.

I've learned that I still have a lot to learn

- MAYA ANGELOU

@DONKEYONAWAFFLE

Learn

I never did History at school so I'm learning lots as an adult. It's more interesting to me now so I retain the information better. But I've also realised that History at school is very limited. Expanding my knowledge now makes me feel less ignorant, more grateful and have a better understanding of the present because of the past. Subjects that don't appeal to you are difficult to learn about and you may not know where to start so you give up. One tip is to start at the beginning and watch or read things aimed at children - they're more fun, colourful and much less intense. From the environment to politics, you can find something out there in a "lite" version. I spent some of lockdown watching "Maddie and Greg" on YouTube with my children and learnt loads.

What I've always been passionate about is learning about science, I find it fun to get to know our planet and everything on it including us humans! I love teaching my children about what things are called and how things work - from insects in the ground to clouds in the sky.

Learning a second language has been shown to be incredibly beneficial especially to young children. Research shows that it boosts problem-solving, creativity, critical-thinking, listening skills, confidence, memory, concentration and the ability to multitask. These are all personal development reasons, so there are also benefits of connecting with other people and cultures to gain new perspectives as well as opening up job opportunities.

Of course, learning doesn't just have to be mental, it can be learning something physical like dance, sport or DIY and it doesn't matter at what age you start. There's so much choice and for most sports there are beginners' classes for all ages. As a female growing up in the 80s and 90s, I didn't get taught many DIY or life skills. This seems to be changing as more girls are learning about traditionally male trades like mechanics, plumbing, electricity etc.

Tasks to Try:

Firstly, work out and understand what, why and how you want to learn something. Read, watch, learn - something about another culture or generation, new facts or skills.

There are lots of free online courses such as Open University and FutureLearn, as well as thousands of TED talks, podcasts, tutorials on social media etc. Search for terms that you're interested in or have always wanted to know more about e.g., an illness, an animal, and see what you could read or listen to!

Your Notes:

• •

• •

• •

• •

Listen

Listen is an anagram of silent. And coincidentally, one of my favourite song lyrics is from 'The Sound of Silence' by Simon and Garfunkel: "People talking without speaking, people hearing without listening".

Listening is not just hearing someone or something, it's asking open questions, looking people in the eyes, noticing their body language, actively listening without judgement or pre-conceived ideas. The main and hardest part is to listen without thinking how the topic relates back to you, without thinking about and forming what you want to say next. People think they need to have something to say, to be interesting, but it's about being interested. Creating a connection means to talk less and listen more – we have one mouth and two ears! Asking questions and remembering little details can make someone feel special as they're being properly listened to.

Active listening is defined as empathic understanding, unconditional positive regard (which means acceptance and support of a person), and a sense of congruence or harmony. It can improve social behaviour because perceiving active listening from someone you're talking to is a positive interaction and helps in terms of future dealings with that person. Feeling accepted, compatible and understood improves any experience and activates our reward systems.

Selective or agenda listening is when we filter or distort, so "we hear what we want to hear". When we agenda listen, we may manipulate someone else's comments to add to the negative messages we are feeding ourselves. It's hearing what backs up our emotional state – and this can sometimes mean missing out the positives or missing the point entirely. This can be harmful, judgemental or can lead to defensive behaviour from either side.

When you talk, you're only repeating what you already know. When you listen you may learn something new.

- DALAI LAMA

@DONKEYONAWAFFLE

Listening to a loved one should be easy, but it has its stumbling blocks. Learning about languages of lovecan be really useful. Gary Chapman wrote a book on the various ways we all express and experience love. He named five love languages people use with partners, family and close friends and when we listen to their language it enhances our relationship with them. They are the ways we express our love as well as how we like to have love expressed to us:

Words of Affirmation – positive communication, gratitude and compliments
Acts of Service – doing thoughtful things or favours
Receiving Gifts – buying or making presents
Quality Time – doing activities together, listening or giving attention
Physical Touch – intimacy, hugging, massage

People use each one in different ways and with varying degrees of priority but they may not be aware of this or how others express their love. E.g., partner A may think spending quality time together is the best form of expressing love and rarely texts or buys gifts but partner B thinks daily compliments, texts and buying gifts shows their love best but doesn't put much time aside to do things together. They both think they're showing their love perfectly but neither is receiving it in their preferred way and begins to think their partner doesn't love them.

An anagram of listen is... silent

Tasks to Try:

Make a conscious effort this week to actively listen, using all the points above. Go into conversations thinking you'll learn something. But try not to have an agenda.

Work out which love languages you prefer and write them down in order of priority. If you have a partner, get them to do the same. Learning how important each one is to you and your partner, how much you use, prefer and expect to receive of each language - will help you understand each other. It can create a stronger bond in your relationship as you can learn to speak each other's language.

Your Notes:

. . . .

. . . .

. . . .

. . . .

Massage

I'm a baby massage instructor so I teach parents how to massage their babies and also talk about the huge benefits of massage to anyone giving or receiving it. This includes pets, not just people! The simple act of touch on a person has a huge impact – the Touch topic goes into more detail on this specifically. Massage is so much more than touch, especially when it's skin to skin, with someone you are close with or if you're receiving massage for a specific reason like an illness or trauma.

There's lots of research that demonstrates that massage affects our hormones to relax and diminish stress. It can increase serotonin and dopamine by about 30% each and decreases cortisol by 30%. Massage also affects the oxytocin system which activates painkilling endorphins so helps reduce pain, fatigue and improves sleep. Sleep is a great benefit in terms of baby massage, for the baby and parents!

Massage gently stimulates and helps our internal systems such as our digestive, respiratory, circulatory and lymphatic systems. (The lymphatic system gets rid of toxins and waste as well as producing immune cells). Massage can release strain and knots in our muscles or aid muscle recovery after sports or injury. It can improve congestion by opening and relaxing the chest. It can encourage drainage of toxins, food to flow in the right direction and blood to circulate efficiently and to where it's needed.

There are hundreds of studies which have shown massage helps with a wide variety of medical issues. These include skin conditions, pain syndromes including arthritis and fibromyalgia, hypertension, autoimmune conditions including asthma and multiple sclerosis, immune conditions including HIV and breast cancer and aging problems including Parkinson's and dementia.

With someone close to you such as your partner or baby, massage is a method

Massage:
Relax the mind
Renew the body
Revive the soul

@DONKEYONAWAFFLE

of bonding so improves interaction, communication and connection. This is the best part of being a baby massage instructor - seeing babies look into their parents' eyes and the intense love between them. I'm also a huge animal lover and there is lots of research surrounding the similar benefits of bonding and connecting with a pet. This is talked about more in the Touch topic.

A secondary part of massage is conditioning your skin with oils. There's a lot of goodness in oils such as coconut oil which reduces inflammation, keeps skin moisturized and helps heal wounds. The fatty acids found in coconut oil also possess antimicrobial properties that can help treat acne and protect the skin from harmful bacteria.

The ancient practice of self-massage (which is called abhyanga) is also an option which is overlooked or not known about. It can feel weird to begin with, but it promotes tissue health, good sleep, soothes the mind and clears toxins. Self-massage therapy is also studied in conditions such as the management of knee osteoarthritis and improves symptoms like pain, stiffness and functional movement.

Tasks to Try:

If you have a partner or best friend you're tactile with, give each other a shoulder or hand massage if you're both willing. Plan when you can give or receive a massage soon, as a treat to yourself or to someone close to you.

Try self-massage - light a scented candle, warm some oils and massage them into your skin, especially your feet (unless you're very ticklish!).

Your Notes:

A
B
C

Mindfulness

This is a well-known term nowadays, it is being present and observing in the moment. There's a saying of "smell the flowers" so it's about really noticing things that you don't normally in your busy life, which slows and calms your body down. Being mindful is being aware of your surroundings, your body, your breathing, and having a few moments in silence or calm sounds. Really noticing every movement, sound, using all the senses. Mindfulness isn't about distraction, but acceptance. It can remove us from overthinking and into feeling: body, breath and sensations.

When exposed to a loud noise, or in expectation of it, cortisol floods our bodies, making us feel on edge. Imagine standing on the side of a road in a city with tons of traffic, people, blaring out all sorts of sounds that merge into one blur. Then switch to suddenly being up a mountain, surrounded by the silence of cool, crisp air. The relief of the quiet and goodness of the fresh environment immediately relaxes you.

One popular relaxation method is to think about your body, starting at your feet, how they are placed on the floor or on the bed. Then work your way up your body thinking about your shins, thighs, stomach, chest, arms, neck and finally head. Then repeat the process but at each body part, try becoming tense to then relax. Tense your feet for 5 seconds, then relax. Work your way to your legs, buttocks, stomach, arms, hands, jaw. Your muscles will find it easier to relax themselves and you're more conscious of the feeling of relaxing them. You may want to keep your eyes closed as you do this to help you concentrate.

There's a breathing technique called Piko-Piko that comes from Hawaii where "Piko" means "navel" or "centre". This exercise is simple:

1) Get into a relaxed position.

2) As you inhale through your nose, imagine you are wearing a crown on

Mindfulness

the top of your head and focus your
attention on that crown.

3) As you exhale through your mouth, shift your attention to your navel.

4) As you inhale and exhale switch your attention from the crown of your head to
your navel. Repeat this three or four times.The act of breathing deeply and
focussing on a particular area and then switching your attention to another spot
helps to relax your mind and reenergise your body.

Making a conscious effort to smell lovely smells that you normally take for
granted can be a mindfulness method. Smell the spices before you add them to
your cooking, smell the toast as it pops, smell some flowers, light a scented
candle, wash your towels and linen with extra powder or put them out to dry
outside, smell the conditioner before washing your hair. Just take time to
consciously use your smelling sense! You can create a positive feeling at home
with fruit, bread, peppermint or other essential oils you love.

Another method for using your senses is the 'Five Things' approach – when you
feel stressed or angry, just notice and list in your head, five things you can see,
five things to touch, five things to smell, five things you can hear.

Tasks to Try:

Look up some meditation tracks, through a specific website, on YouTube or an app. I'd highly recommend trying a few different ones and so see which voice you like the best. If you find the voice cringey or irritating, look for another one as the voice is key to your enjoyment and the effectiveness of mindfulness. The main three points to try are:

1) Recognise your thoughts, all of them coming in and out your mind.

2) Settle your mind, breathe deeply and notice your thoughts coming in but watch them pass as you bring yourself back to focusing on your breathing.

3) Repeat 1 and 2 for 5 mins each – the repetition improves how well you focus and relax.

Your Notes:

Mistakes

Most of us have a persona, meaning a face we don't mind people seeing. It's made up of the traits that we have on display for others, so they form an image in their mind of what they think about us and who we are to them. We're also likely to have aspects of ourselves or our lives that we think of as private, some of which may be so people don't see our faults, failings or mistakes.

If you think back to something you have failed at, note the feelings that may come to mind – they're bound to be mostly negative such as disappointing, embarrassing, guilty and even mortifying. Failure is viewed as a negative experience and we tend to judge ourselves as a person rather than looking at that stand-alone action that failed. Simply disassociating ourselves as a whole with whatever we think we've failed at can be the first step to feeling better and not being so harsh on yourself. And this is the case whether you have low expectations of yourself, (so you may not push yourself in case you fail) or you have unrealistically high expectations (so you may never reach what you want to achieve and always feel like you're failing).

A museum trip I remember with my dad, was where we learned about the inventor, Thomas Edison, who famously said, "I have not failed. I've just found 10,000 ways that won't work", before he was successful in inventing the light bulb. This is reflected in the neuro-linguistic programming (NLP) phrase, "There's no such thing as failure, just feedback". Failure is such a strong, unhelpful and negative word, a better way to think of any mistakes or unsuccessful attempts are as opportunities to learn. It's much more helpful to see problems as challenges not threats.

There's no such thing as failure, just feedback

@DONKEYONAWAFFLE

Everyone makes mistakes, even the people you look up to the most. Hundreds of things were invented by mistake; penicillin, fireworks, Velcro, microwaves, superglue to name a few. We grow from our mistakes and it shows strength when we say sorry.

It also takes peace to forgive yourself – and others.

When you feel resentment, anger or upset, your body produces stress hormones. In general, nobodypurposely hurts another and if we understand that, it is easier to forgive. It is also important that we forgive ourselves and it is a reminder that we are not perfect. Forgiveness is a great antidote to pessimism and relieves the stress.

Regret is inescapable but by understanding what kind of choices you regret the most, you can learn from them for the future. In terms of the past, all our experiences shape who we are, so there's a good chance that some of the ones we regret play a role in the things we value today. In terms of the future, we can accept the fact we all have limits and not every single dream we have may come true, it's just being realistic and takes the pressure and disappointment away. Imagine yourself at 90 years old, what would you like to look back on and say that you've done? Or at your funeral, what would you wish people would say about you and your life? Start living it that way and you'll certainly never regret it.

If you're a parent, it's a great thing to show your children that you're not perfect, you make mistakes, and when you do, you're kind to yourself. Children mimic their parents, so if you're hard on yourself when making a mistake, then they will be too.

Tasks to Try:

Reframe the past – this doesn't mean pretending something didn't happen, but you can find meaning or positive things that have come out of regrettable experiences. What did you learn, did you become more resilient, empathetic or did you meet someone important?

Write a letter to younger self – as a child or a teenager. Imagine what you may write in 10-20 years' time to yourself now.

For a bit of fun, do a search on your idols or famous people that have 'failed' but who kept persevering or trying something different before they became successful.

Your Notes:

Motivation

Motivation flows on nicely from mistakes, as you may need to motivate yourself to do something which you have failed at in the past or have a feeling you'll give up on from fear of failure or some other reason.

Most people have a good idea of what is good for them in terms of health, work and habits. It's not a lack of information that's the problem, but a combination of procrastination, lack of follow-through and self-control. In general, it seems we want to do what we know is good for us. Just not right now.

During the covid-19 lockdown, many people found it a huge struggle to get motivated. My husband was one of the only people I know who lost weight and increased his fitness. During that time, most people did the opposite, understandably. Uncertain times affect us all in different ways but lack of motivation is incredibly common. There are days when you won't want to take action and that's OK. However, if you're stressed about your lack of motivation, this can have an impact on your mental health and well-being.

Motivation is a flow, it's not an on-off switch and there's normally a driving force behind it, a reason, a purpose. When you accomplish any of these purposes, acknowledging and even celebrating your wins, however big or small is a great practice to get into. All the little wins count and they create that spark in us. You're the creator of how you want to tackle your days and what you want to accomplish.

The Habits and Goals topic lists methods people use to form habits. One way specific to motivation is to involve another person. Most people fit into a personality trait where we often break promises to ourselves, but rarely do to others as we'd feel awful letting them down. If you have someone to check in with weekly or

do something with that person, you're much more likely to feel motivated and stick to your plan. One extreme example is if you want to stick to a gym schedule, swap a gym shoe with your friend at the end of the session so you have to turn up to the next one for them to be able to exercise! If you can't think of anyone then just the simple act of writing down your goals can boost your motivation and increase the likelihood you'll reach your goal by 50%.

One emotion that is actually helpful for motivation is anxiety – but with the right amount. Too much and we freeze, too little and we become complacent. We perform at our best with a certain level of anxiety, which varies from person to person. So instead of aiming to get rid of anxiety, we can know that it is useful so we can work with it, but not let it take control. It then won't hinder our motivation, but help it.

Motivation is much more productive when coupled with kindness. The intent behind the motivation needs to come from a place of care. If you're motivating yourself or someone else is motivating you with force or shame then it won't be good for your well-being.

Try not to put pressure on yourself about needing to know what you're going to do with the rest of your life right now, whatever age you are. Most people who were sure of their career path at 20 are having midlife crises in their 40s. However, it is important to find a balance. We don't want to neglect our future selves as we may not want to believe or be able to imagine ourselves getting old. Taking time to picture yourself in years to come – what you look like, what you're doing, where you're living, who is around you – may encourage you to change your behaviour today, for the sake of that future self. E.g., imagining yourself retired may make you think more about sorting out a pension.

Tasks to Try:

Write down a list of things you want to do, change or achieve in the next 6 months or year. These could be small like baking your first cake or big like an exercise plan or learning a new skill. Write how you can achieve these goals and what motivation you need to do to reach them.

These three questions can help with everyday motivation:

1) What do I want today to be about?

2) What action do I need to take?

3) How will I feel at the end of the day once I've accomplished this?

Your Notes:

· ·

· ·

· ·

· ·

A
B
C

Move

We all know that exercise is good for our physical and mental health, but it's easy to be reluctant as it feels like the benefits are so far away, or "being healthier" is such a vague aim. Instead of having goals of lowering your blood pressure, losing weight or getting fit, which seem like a long (and sometimes boring!) road, think about it in the short term. Eg if you go for a jog or do yoga at home, it will make you more energised for when you see your friends later, or pick up your children, or have that meeting. Just 3 minutes of movement affects your feel-good hormones, stress hormones, metabolism, mood and of course muscle strength and the health of your organs.

Movement doesn't just mean exercise. If you don't like traditional exercise or haven't got much time, dance while going about your day! Studies have shown dancing helps with dementia, Parkinson's, cerebral palsy amongst many other illnesses. It gives a sense of togetherness if you're dancing in a group as you relate to each other and move in sync to the same beat.

Or just walk... On average, people are sitting for 9.3 hours a day which is more than we sleep (average of 7.7 hours a day). Like most forms of exercise, the benefits of walking include increased cardiovascular (heart) and pulmonary (lung) health, stronger bones and muscles, reduced body fat, improved balance and endurance, decreased fatigue. As well as these physical aspects, there are huge benefits to our brains - walking can improve creativity, memory and mood. It encourages our brain to release endorphins that boost mental health, decrease sensitivity to stress and pain, and can make us feel euphoric. Walking also increases the production of Brain-Derived Neurotrophic Factor (BDNF), which is a protein that is essential for neuronal development and cognitive function.

Respect your body.
Fuel your body.
Challenge your body.
Move your body.
And most of all...
LOVE your body

@DONKEYONAWAFFLE

Increased blood flow and therefore oxygen to the brain is another advantage. Our brains use about 20%

of our body's total oxygen supply, so if we're not getting enough oxygen up there, it's easy to feel 'foggy' or unfocused. Increased blood flow to the brain is linked to better cognitive function, improved memory and overall protection against decline. Walking keeps your heart beating, blood circulating and lungs breathing, your brain engages in constant 'cognitive mapping' when you walk. This can be summed up as our 'internal GPS', the process that keeps you basically oriented with a sense of where major landmarks are and which direction you need to go. When you walk, your brain is doing this without your awareness.

Neuroscientist Shane O'Mara describes the brain as 'motor-centric', saying it evolved to support movement, so if we stop moving about, it won't work as well. Walking is much more accessible than other forms of exercise as you don't need equipment, a membership and there's very little risk because it's not high impact or stressful on your body.

Wordsworth composed poetry as he wandered, while Aristotle delivered lectures on foot in the grounds of his school in Athens. The philosopher Friedrich Nietzsche memorably said that "only thoughts reached by walking have value", a notion that Charles Dickens - who was as prolific a walker as he was a writer - would no doubt have seconded.

Every day brings a chance for you to draw in a breath, kick off your shoes and dance

- Oprah Winfrey

@DONKEYONAWAFFLE

Tasks to Try:

This week, could you change a meeting with someone (social or work) into a walk-and-talk meeting instead of a seated meeting?

Can you take the stairs instead of a lift?

Could you park further away or get off the bus earlier?

Can you walk a neighbour's dog?

Try to be in nature if possible, not looking at your phone. Even if for 10 mins a day, walk in fresh air whatever the weather!

Your Notes:

· ·

· ·

· ·

· ·

A
B
C

Music

Music has some serious scientific benefits for our health and overall well-being. Not only can it soothe a broken heart, motivate a workout and bring people together, but it can improve memory function, sleep quality, increase rates of healing and act as a powerful stress management tool.

Listening to music can have a tremendously relaxing effect on our minds and bodies. Slow music with simple melody and no lyrics, can have a beneficial effect on our physiological functions, slowing the pulse and heart rate, lowering blood pressure, decreasing the levels of stress hormones and muscle tension. These effects have been shown after a listening time of 13 minutes. When listening to fast music with positive lyrics, only 9 minutes of music is required to make people feel uplifted.

Other research has studied the following areas:

<u>Music improves health</u>

A study called Music as Medicine, tested 7,581 participants and found that 89% believed music to be essential for their health and well-being. With slow music, 90% of participants used music to relax, 81.8% used it to make them feel happy and 46.5% used it to process and/or release sadness. With fast music, 89% had improved energy levels, 65% laughed more and others felt more in control of their lives or able to 'take on anything'.

Music's form and structure can bring order and security to disabled and distressed children. It encourages coordination and communication, so improves their quality of life.

Listening to music on headphones reduces stress and anxiety in hospital patients before and after surgery.

Music

Music can help reduce both the sensation and distress of both chronic pain and postoperative pain. Listening to music can relieve depression and increase self-esteem ratings in elderly people.

Music therapy significantly reduces emotional distress and boosts quality of life among adult cancer patients.

Music improves relationships

Hearing music alters the neurochemicals in our brains and triggers the release of dopamine and endorphins. These neurotransmitters lift our mood and allow us to share a positive chemical rush with the people we're with.

Several studies observing indigenous people who use music in their gatherings, found that listening to music together strengthens the bonds in groups by making people feel they belong and increasing their positive perceptions of the people within their community.

The rhythm of music also synchronizes people- a sway, tap of the foot, nod of the head, or full on dancing - moving in sync with other people makes you in tune with them.

Music sparks nostalgia

Music is the most common way that brings about nostalgia because it ignites your amygdala (which deals with emotions) and hippocampus (which deals with memories) in your brain, sparking joy, excitement, sadness, or even annoyance. It can take you to an exact time, place, or remind you immediately of a person. It's certainly the strongest for me. Many songs can flood me with emotions, positivity and nostalgia. I get goose-bumps within seconds and can easily cry with happiness and feeling moved, if I'm in the right circumstance. There are theories that nostalgia most commonly connects to your adolescence, as there was a lot more brain chemistry floating around at that age with the hormonal changes. So it was easier to form powerful, emotional memories which you later unlock and go back to your teenage years.

Tasks to Try:

This week, listen to old and new music. Music you've not listened to in a while that you love as well as music you don't know. Get friends to send you songs they think you'll like, or their favourite songs and you do the same back. You may find a favourite you've never heard before!

If you're on your own at some point at home, put on some music - maybe from your teenage years - and dance! This could be half dancing while tidying up or sitting at a desk, light dancing when on the phone to a faint beat, or full on crazy in the kitchen while cooking!

Your Notes:

• •

• •

• •

A
B
C

• •

Nature

Wildlife of any kind is good for the soul. Spending time outside, surrounded by nature is such an easy boost but is easily forgotten or dismissed. Walking outside when angry or stressed can activate more areas of the brain which then helps you to think more clearly. Interviews with 20,000 people in England found that people spending two hours or more per week in nature - doing exercise or simply sitting on a bench - are significantly more likely to report good health. The benefits were the same for young, old, wealthy, poor, urban, rural people and for those with long-term illnesses and disabilities.

Being outside or being surrounded by plants can also increase memory retention by up to 20%. The effect of nature stimulates the senses and the mind, improving cognition and performance. When we engage with natural objects like plants and trees we go into a meditative state, it moves our consciousness from one part of the brain to another, so we get some of the effects of meditation simply from being with nature.

David Attenborough said, "15 mins a day simply sitting and watching wildlife boosts our well-being by giving us breathing space from the stresses of daily life".

It's so easy to lose our connection to nature with regards to where our food comes from. Buying food is generally a rush to the supermarket, collecting produce-in-plastic that's often been flown into the country from afar. But how did that food get from farm to fork? Planting, growing, nurturing, picking and then eating your own vegetables, fruits or herbs is a learning and satisfying experience.

Other benefits include reducing plastic packaging, saving money, and even attracting bees and butterflies. All this adds to an increased well-being. Even growing a potted plant in your house is shown to make us happier - watching the plant grow while nurturing it, leads to an emotional boost.

An understanding of the natural world, & what's in it is a source of not only great curiosity but great fulfillment

- DAVID ATTENBOROUGH

@DONKEYONAWAFFLE

If you're not green fingered and want something simpler, easier and quicker for that boost, then look to the sky. Did you ever cloud-spot as a child? Looking for faces, animals and shapes or just appreciating the various patterns and colours of all clouds. It's fun to do by yourself or with people (especially children with their vivid imaginations). When our attention settles and we observe the sky with wonder, we become calmly present in the moment and we slow down.

Walk-and-talk therapy has become more popular and is called 'ecotherapy'. People often feel less apprehensive or awkward outside, compared to a formal setting like a consultation room where you may be face to face with someone. Being side by side means less eye contact so people often feel less exposed so then they talk more openly. If someone doesn't like crying in front of others, walking outdoors means they can look away and absorb the scenery. Walking in nature means that people can be silent without that uncomfortable feeling someone is watching and waiting for you to speak. Silence outdoors is natural and the setting provides so much else to fill the gap. And often, being quiet is crucial to the healing process. Nature is uplifting and enhances our ability to connect with our feelings and inner calm, leading to a more positive mood and way of thinking.

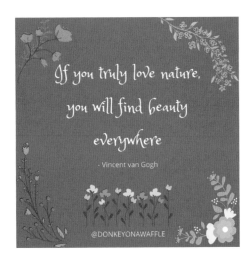

If you truly love nature, you will find beauty everywhere

- Vincent van Gogh

@DONKEYONAWAFFLE

Tasks to Try:

If you can't get out in nature in the next week, plan a day when you can. Try having your bare feet on the grass, eating outside, having a walk while chatting instead of sitting inside. Be mindful and appreciate the trees, leaves, flowers, clouds and any colours, smells and sounds of any birds etc.

Make a bird feeder or bath. (Despite their feathers cooling them down, birds get hot and thirsty too). When you see one coming to what you've made it'll no doubt make you smile!

Your Notes:

A
B
C

Old School Ways

As a culture, we've become incredibly focused on convenience and saving time (and time is money). We also spend a lot of time trying to improve ourselves. But sometimes this means missing out on pleasures and the 'old' way of doing things. Things we love or treat ourselves with, can become a guilty pleasure but why not take the guilt out of it and instead of trying to be better and save time and work harder... we try to experience more pleasure. Self-improvement and enjoyment should go hand in hand, not against each other. E.g., if you're deciding to eat healthily, you can still make the meal a treat by lighting candles and savouring each bite with pleasure. If you're deciding to exercise, find something that you enjoy like dancing or doing a sport with a friend so it's not a chore or hard slog.

By going back to the old school ways of doing things like browsing in a shop, you may discover something new to try or find a perfect gift for someone you would never have seen. Seeing and smelling fruit or cheese may steer you to cooking or eating something different to normal. Touching and trying on clothes with a friend is spending quality time with them. Buying online often means things don't fit or aren't what you expected, and returning items is costly and extra effort. Physically going to a shop may work both ways, but for some, it means buying more consciously rather than the ease of clicking away behind a screen. Of course for some it means buying more, so there's finding the right balance for you.

Most of us have smart phones which enable us to take thousands of photos, but how often do we look through them? There are usually so many meaningless or rubbish photos, they dilute the decent ones which therefore aren't easily found. It takes a fair bit of time and effort, but deleting unwanted photos is great for finding those gems again. And even better, print some favourites into a photobook or collage so you can appreciate them every day. Making photo collages of holidays, festivals, weddings etc. is fun, keeps

I saw this and thought of you

@DONKEYONAWAFFLE

the memories alive and they make great, personal gifts. Old school ways can also be about realising what fun things you used to love doing and questioning why you don't do them anymore. There may be something you're able to do, but now you say "I used to… go dancing, play board games, go camping, socialise, play sport". Replacing "I used to" with "I will…" can make that small difference to motivating you to go back to an old school way and reigniting that enjoyment.

Tasks to Try:

Doing something the old school way just for a change this week may inspire you, feel refreshing or bring you in contact with people you wouldn't have otherwise. It can be physically going into a shop rather than buying online, or calling someone you'd normally text, or getting a solid board game out instead of playing computer games.

Everyone loves receiving nice post, so sending out real invitations to a party or a letter rather than an email can be a lovely surprise. "I saw this and thought of you" was a slogan in the 1990s and is such a kind idea. It's simply sending something thoughtful or personal in the post to someone. The old school way shows effort and thought. It could be a magazine or newspaper article, a funny picture or a small present, something to make them smile.

Your Notes:

Plan

Planning is bringing the future into the present. The benefits of better success are talked about in business a lot but this is more about life outside of work. It's about having something to look forward to – just having a social event in the diary can spark joy. Some people aren't planners, which is fine. It could be a case of trying it out to see if it lifts you or makes things easier, but not if it causes stress. The best way is to plan an activity when you're feeling good, not when you're tired or down. Although it's a common thing to plan your next holiday or festival as soon as you're back from the last to cure the post-holiday blues!

Getting organised and planning can help to avoid future stress. Knowing that you're prepared for something, having a plan B or methods in place that are a "just in case" can minimise the likelihood of things going wrong or even a catastrophe. There's a cute saying: "If plan A doesn't work, the alphabet has 25 more letters"!

Being locked out your house in the middle of the night or when just back from a trip with hungry children in the car could be a nightmare. However, if you've planned for such a frustrating time, and given a key to someone nearby or installed a key safe box hidden in the garden, then this could save a whole load of hassle and despair.

When we're stressed we release cortisol which causes many bodily systems to shut down. This happens for evolutionary reasons – when faced with a predator, humans didn't need their digestive system, libido or immune system for example. We didn't use energy on these systems, as reactions were more important – so energy went to breathing deeply, and getting oxygen and glucose to our muscles to run. Rational logical thinking also goes out the window when we're stressed as we made quick decisions that aren't always thought out to consider the options and possible outcomes. So a quick and bad decision could be made when faced with a stressful situation, which could have been avoided with

Hindsight, we're told, is a wonderful thing.

But hindsight in advance is even better

@DONKEYONAWAFFLE

a bit of planning ahead. To combat the cloudy thinking when we're stressed, we can use "prospective hindsight" or "premortem", a technique invented by psychologist Gary Klein. It's about looking ahead and figuring out which things could go wrong and putting methods in place to minimise these potential mini disasters. One example is designating a place for items that are commonly lost in your house like glasses, wallet, keys or passport. This sounds silly but for some people it could be a very useful and simple change that saves time and stress. Another example is taking photos of your passport and credit card when you travel and emailing these to yourself, which may help if they get lost or stolen when abroad. One last example is thinking about if you get ill or have an accident, plan what your decisions would be around medical care and quality of life. Practising this kind of thinking may make the decision easier when it comes to it.

Tasks to Try:

Make a few plans, write out what your decisions would be for financial, medical or social situations. You can look at "what if..." questions like "what if I get locked out of my car or my car breaks down". Another way is to look back at past situations that were stressful and what avoidance methods could've been put in place – and check if those methods are in place now!

Your Notes:

• •

• •

A
B
C

• •

• •

Play

Playing (outside of playing sports) is normally associated with children. In the mid-century, and sadly in some parts of the world now, children as young as five worked so they didn't really have a childhood filled with playing. We then moved away from that to children playing all day by themselves in the woods, back in time for dinner. In more recent years however, there's been a trend back towards less play and more 'work' in the way of scheduling - structured classes of music, sport and hobbies - which isn't the free play which can be so important for children and adulthood. Free play is unstructured and unsupervised, so it's when children have the chance to make up their games with their own rules. This way they learn to negotiate and share through their own experiences rather than being told or shown by an adult. Free play promotes creativity, cognitive language, social, emotional and self-regulation skills that build executive function. Executive functions are key to becoming a well-rounded adult as they include problem solving, collaboration, planning, memory and self-control.

Growing up doesn't mean we have to leave play behind. My dad's always had a games room which I've now adopted the idea of too, but I'm aware not every household is like this. Christmas time is usually the time of year when board games are played, but why not other times? Hectic lifestyles don't give us time or we just forget about these types of games (or maybe it's because they cause arguments!). Aside from any disagreements or competitiveness that gets out of hand, playing games can invite something a bit different to a normal evening or weekend and can invoke ideas, fun, as well as using your brain. Research shows that play can help trauma recovery, relieve stress, improve brain function and enhance relationships. However, we shouldn't play specifically with these points in mind, we have to play for the enjoyment, without aiming for a goal of improvement. Allowing yourself to live in the moment of play, without any pressure of having to excel at an activity is the key, so playing as a toddler would. I remember my friend's

son, making a whole game out of a coat-hanger which was so free-spirited, imaginative and hilarious! When we're stressed, we can't tell our minds what to think, but we can tell our minds what to do. So an activity that stretches the mind enough, grabs your attention and makes you feel good will mean you're engaged in a different activity, away from stress. Your focus is in a game, not on your problems. Of course, this can turn into being a bad thing if you are always escaping into a game and not facing any of your problems. Games have to be in moderation - they can be a great escape to deal with a mind that's spinning but shouldn't be an avoidance strategy.

The video game industry is worth more than the film and music industries together, so many people are doing this already but there's obviously the associated risks and worries of isolation and addiction. There are various ways that games can reward the brain and therefore release dopamine. Games measure progress, set multiple short and long term aims, give rewards for small and big efforts, respond with feedback for improved learning, include elements of exciting uncertainty, and improve confidence, courage, attention and memory.

Tasks to Try:

Play a board game, cards, verbal game, even if just once this week. You could get an old game out the back of the cupboard, buy one you used to have as a child from a charity shop, or simply use paper and pen to play battleships!

Your Notes:

• •

• •

A
B
C

• •

• •

Positivity

Being positive by exercising, meditating, showing gratitude, being kind etc., can rewire your brain and can mean you're more likely to be happy and then successful. The mistake is thinking that working hard = success = happiness, but this often doesn't work as what does 'success' mean? Most of us move the goal posts of success, so even when we succeed at something, we then strive to achieve the next thing, so happiness is always being reached for and it comes back to the "I'll be happy when..." or "IF.... then I'll be happy". Our brains work the opposite way. When we are positive, our creativity, energy and learning all increase, and we're *then* more successful.

It can be instinctive to be negative and think "typical" if something goes wrong. But why is it typical? Why not think of all the things that have gone well today instead? How we respond to the information around us is reflected in our emotions and behaviour. It is estimated that through our five senses, our nervous system is bombarded with two million bits of data each second of each day. We can only make sense of about seven manageable chunks per second. The reticular activating system (RAS) in our brain filters the rest of the data by deleting, distorting or generalising information. The bits that get filtered depend on our individual values, beliefs, internal guidelines, memories and experiences. So one scenario is experienced differently by each person who is there, because everyone's mind works differently.

The RAS receives these bits of information from our conscious mind and passes them onto our unconscious mind. When you think of a goal, you may consciously create a representation of it with pictures, sounds, feelings, even tastes and smells. These ideas are passed onto your unconscious mind and help you achieve your goal by bringing to your attention all the relevant information which may have otherwise been taken away or ignored. One example is

when you're about to buy a car, and have a make and model in mind, you suddenly see that same model everywhere. Another example is when you hear someone saying your name from the other side of a noisy room. Your brain is filtering through these millions of bits of information and decides which ones are most important to you. We hear what we want to hear and we see what we want to see.

So, if you think negatively, or even if you use negative words when you're trying to think positively, your RAS will focus on those thoughts and it will become a self-fulfilling prophecy or self-sabotage. E.g., if you tell yourself when you're about to do a speech in public, "Don't panic if everyone stares at you" or "I'm so worried I won't get the promotion" your RAS focuses on those words: panicking / everyone staring at you / worrying / not getting the promotion. The RAS works to prove our beliefs right, so if you change to thinking positively, happier beliefs are reinforced.

Affirmations are positive statements that, when repeated, can help you to overcome negative thoughts. My favourites are:

"I have the confidence and strength to conquer my challenges"
"I have the potential to succeed"
"Today is going to be good day"

By repeating affirmations regularly, you can start to increase positive thinking. You can have your affirmations written at your desk, as your phone screensaver or even sing them to yourself, as singing activates more of your brain so cements it even more. Look for the positives and what is going right. Expecting good things to happen will lead to taking actions that produce positive results. Seeing the glass half full not only makes you happier, it makes you healthier.

Tasks to Try:

If you have negative thoughts appear this week, ask yourself what is the reality, and look at the facts. What would you advise your friend if they were thinking this? Think about what you can do instead of what you can't. Use positive language and your unconscious will work with you.

Write down thoughts and positive affirmations and say them (or sing them!) out loud repeatedly. Then slowly, your RAS will alter what it presents to your conscious.

Your Notes:

· ·

· ·

A
B
C

· ·

· ·

Relationships

People generally feel happier and benefit from stress relief after catching up with friends. The "Roseto effect" is a phenomenon that showed that close connections within a community, which include kindness and support, provided a cardio-protective effect. It was from a US census in 1960 that found no one under 45 years old in the town of Roseto had ever died of heart disease, and the death rate for over 65s was less than half the national average. So it suggests that having nurturing relationships is good for your heart.

However, socialising isn't for everyone all the time, especially us introverts. A 2019 study on happiness and social behaviour in 30,000 people states that links between happiness and social behaviour are more complex than often assumed.

Studies that look at various influences of peoples' overall well-being, suggest that age, gender, salary and even health issues don't make a difference to happiness. The factor that has the biggest effect is having meaningful relationships.

When covid-19 hit, most people massively missed the social side of seeing friends and family. Most of us are so lucky to have amazing technology like video calling but it's not the same. A lot of people being in lockdown with family meant they spent more quality time together instead of filling the weekends full of social events. A lot of people did lots of family activities they've always thought of but not had time.

However, there is also heavy strain on relationships when spending much more time together – especially without much choice. Communication is the key to any relationship, whether it's a partner, child, friend or colleague. Saying your piece can be important, and aiming to express your values is key, rather than being right. Bringing up a problem can be tough but what makes it easier is focusing on their behaviour, not them as a person, e.g., "I don't like the way you walk out the

It's not what you have in life that matters, But who you have in life that counts

@DONKEYONAWAFFLE

room when I'm still talking" instead of "you're selfish, arrogant and inconsiderate". Trying to understand where the other person is coming from is also important, by asking them questions and listening to them properly. Allowing someone to express themselves may help them see the issue differently and may also let you reconsider your own views. Most behaviours have a positive intent - meaning there's usually something positive that a person is trying to achieve. Even if a behaviour seems negative, searching for the reason behind it can help ease any conflict. E.g., grandma giving your child sugar at bedtime may seem irresponsible and disrespectful to your wishes, but her intent was to be loved by your child. Showing yourself compassion after a conflict is also key. Amends can be made and people who love you should respect the fact you've expressed what's true for you.

Tasks to Try:

This week, get in touch with a family member, an old friend or colleague, to ask how they're doing. People sometimes think it's awkward if it's been left too long but life gets in the way and it's nice to reconnect. The most likely response you'll get is "how lovely to hear from you!" If there's no one you can think of, is there a work colleague or neighbour you could get to know more?

Talk instead of type - pick a few texts or emails you're about to write and call that person instead. It may actually save time if it's going to be a conversation and questions. It's more personal, it may mean you interpret things better and you may learn something you wouldn't have otherwise.

Your Notes:

· ·

· ·

A
B
C

· ·

· ·

Resilience

Someone described to me two analogies of what being resilient is and I think they're great ways to explain, especially to a child:

1) Imagine a pitched tent in a field with the most incredible winds. Gusts of air are lashing against the sides, the speed of the wind is shaking the guide ropes and the whole thing is dancing. But it's resilient and stays standing tall, despite everything that's against it.

2) Picture a garden lawn full of daisies and dandelions. You mow the lawn so it's all neat and short, with the flowers gone. Then the next day the daisies and dandelions are back, popping up everywhere above the cut grass, showing how strong and resilient they are even after being knocked down by a huge, sharp metal machine!

The language used in both examples can be used for people who show resilience when they come up against something or someone who is trying to blow or knock them over or mow them down. Resisting the attack, letting it go over your head and standing tall are all ways to stay strong.

Resilience is the capacity to recover from a difficult time or place and to bounce back from that struggle, coming out stronger and wiser. It's about maintaining our mental health and well-being while continuing essential tasks. In the face of a crisis or tragedy, finding a sense of purpose can play an important role in your recovery. Finding something that resonates with you that's meaningful will build that resilience so you can cope. The Healing topic talks more about this.

Sometimes there's an assumption that resilience is when you keep going on and on without dropping anything, but that is endurance, which can lead to burnout. Resilience involves making

I am not what happened to me,
I am what I choose to become

- CARL JUNG

@DONKEYONAWAFFLE

adaptions to decide what really needs doing. This means prioritising tasks and having honest conversations with people that may want you to continue doing things, like your boss or family. Highly resilient people usually have a high level of self-awareness. They understand and manage their emotions in a positive way as well as taking responsibility for their thoughts and behaviour. Resilient people find meaning in the lives they live. An optimistic attitude usually works better than being pessimistic. So when we accept that life can be a challenge, but know that these challenges are tolerable, bearable and will pass, we're building resilience for any future challenges. Reframing is a great skill to develop. By reframing your situation in positive terms, it becomes easier to see how you grow and learn from your experiences.

The Kindness and Mistakes topics both mention resilience because being kind to others (and ourselves) and making mistakes, makes us more resilient. As does a strong social network and humour!

My experiences in life – the people I've met, the places I've been to, the jobs I've had, my family, the good and bad things that have happened, the mistakes I've made – have taught me so many things. It's more often the bad things that give you the opportunity to stop, reflect, learn and grow. And these things enable you to become more resilient and to be the person you want to be and create the life that you love.

Tasks to Try:

Reflect on your difficult times and challenges in the past, and discover hidden resilient qualities you may have forgotten you have.

Ask yourself:

- What did you experience and what did this teach you?

- What did you learn about yourself and how did you change?

- How is this reflected in your life today?

Your Notes:

Self-Care

Self-care is about looking after yourself physically, mentally and spiritually. It's about doing things to be kind to yourself, and can be interchangeable with self-compassion which focuses more on how you think about yourself. Both are about alleviating suffering in yourself by taking action or protecting yourself. Studies show that self-care and self-compassion are associated with happiness and mindfulness.

70-80% of people are harsher on themselves than they are to others. Being kind to yourself with the same care as you would naturally show to a friend is hard to do but is greatly important to practise self-care. When you face a battle or conflict of any sort, would you want a critical voice in your head or one of a supportive ally? Choosing the right voice makes a powerful change to your outlook, actions and self-worth. Studies show that there's an inherent connection between self-worth and being amongst people, as we gain the perspective and awareness that other people struggle too and that it's OK to ask for help. So it's the opposite of having self-pity, where you may catastrophize your problems and feel that bad things only happens to you.

We all have an inner critic and usually it's worse than any judgement or words we hear from others around us. If we look at what's behind these internal messages, this can help us understand and then manage them if need be. Usually self-criticism serves to protect or push. Protecting from failure, rejection, pain or a

negative experience or pushing ourselves out of our comfort zone or to improve ourselves. However, this self-criticism can become so strong that it takes over and becomes limiting. If you know that your inner critic is just a part of you that is trying to protect you, you can accept this and address other parts of you, such as courage, confidence and growth, which you can allow to take control. So alongside a bit of healthy criticism and self-challenge, you have

Self-Care

that self-care, compassion and kindness. One of my favourite pieces of advice is to talk to yourself like the person who loves you the most would. Or talk to yourself like you would talk to your best friend. Treating yourself is the enjoyment side of self-care that we get sold, like a massage or a weekend away - these things are still amazing to do and can be fantastic for your well-being. They can reset, refresh and rejuvenate, but they're temporary self-care solutions. Trying to live your life so self-care is a normal part of everyday is vital.

Author Brianna Wiest says, "Self-care is often a very unbeautiful thing. True self-care is not all salt baths and chocolate cake, it is making the choice to build a life you don't need to regularly escape from." This can mean doing something that feels uncomfortable, like telling a toxic friend you can't meet up (see the Boundaries topic). It is taking the pressure off yourself, being kind to yourself and in fact aiming to be average rather than exceptional. Wiest summarises, "It means being the hero of your life, not the victim. It is no longer choosing a life that looks good over a life that feels good. It is giving up on some goals so you can care about and focus on other goals. It is being honest even if that means you aren't universally liked."

Self-care is giving the world the best of you, rather than what's left of you

@DONKEYONAWAFFLE

Tasks to Try:

What would your life look life if you were kinder to yourself?

How can you take care of yourself (rather than "fix" yourself)?

Try a befriending meditation by showing loving kindness towards yourself. Sit tall and breathe deeply. Choose your own words similar to "I am enough. I promise to be kind to myself in this moment. I wish to be healthy, safe and happy. I deeply and totally love and accept myself." It will feel weird at first but practising makes the mind stronger and your brain will absorb the words.

Your Notes:

• •

• •

• •

A
B
C

• •

Senses

Our five senses are sight, hearing, taste, smell and touch. If we're lucky enough to have all five, it's common to take them for granted or use them without much thought. All the senses can create incredibly strong emotions from contentment and euphoria to anger and stress.

Sounds can set off all sorts of emotions, which is talked about in the Music topic in more detail. But it's not just music that produces reactions, other sounds like someone's voice, the waves of the sea on a beach, a lawn mower, an animal's cry, a siren or alarm - all these can evoke an immediate reaction whether it's good or bad.

Using pleasant scents to enhance well-being dates back thousands of years. Fragrant oils were used for ancient ceremonies in the Far East, Egypt and Greece. Essential oils were extracted from herbs and flowers for making medicines and perfumes. Aromas can evoke a response in an instant, like walking passed your favourite restaurant or bakery, smelling freshly cut grass, getting a wave of a perfume that reminds you of someone or nuzzling your baby's head. A newborn's odour contains about 150 different chemicals and causes a surge of dopamine in the mother as well as increasing the feelings of bonding and protection, so sniffing our babies encourages us to stay close to them.

Aromatherapy or scent therapy has become really popular in recent years and can be extremely powerful to some people. Several studies have shown essential oils such as lavender and rose can reduce stress. Lavender is also linked to improved sleep, increased peripheral blood flow (associated with relaxation) and decreased blood pressure. The smells associated with eating or walking in nature can be "aromatherapeutic" even without deliberately introducing a specific scent.

"These are a few of my

Favourite Things..."

@DONKEYONAWAFFLE

Pleasant aromas can be used to pair up that scent with a desired feeling like calmness, confidence, happiness etc. It can be unconscious, e.g., on a relaxing spa day you may be exposed to certain fragrances, and then when you smell them again, it elicits a relaxation response. Or it can be a conscious act. You can consciously smell a scent (that you don't already associate with anything) at a time when you're feeling in a good or desired state. Doing so may link the experience of that state with the scent sufficiently so that in the future, exposure to the scent may be enough to bring back those feelings. This is called anchoring or associative learning as you're associating a smell with a feeling: a specific aroma triggers a response in you. Anchors can be sounds, touch, words, but using smell and sound seem to be the most powerful and long-lasting as they affect the amygdala and hippocampus so quickly and potently. For me, the powerful smell of coconut sun cream transports me to feeling sunny straight away, and the smell of Chanel no. 5 makes me feel calm as it reminds me of a specific person.

In the same way, taste is often connected to something you ate on a special occasion or a childhood meal your parents cooked you regularly – it's nice to remember delicious foods but sometimes it can be disgusting tastes that stick in your memory. I remember when I was very ill as a child, my mum put liver in a burger to try to get some iron in me. It was so gross I've not eaten a burger since!

Touch is an incredibly powerful sense so has a whole section to itself. As does sight in the Visual section, but just to mention here that the sight of a loved one, a landscape, an animal, a sunset, even a colour can change your mood, thoughts and behaviour instantaneously. When was the last time someone asked what your favourite animal or colour is? Thinking about what you love evokes pleasure, nostalgia and may inspire you to seek out your favourite something.

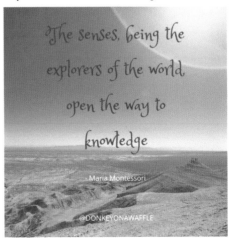
The senses, being the explorers of the world, open the way to knowledge

Maria Montessori

@DONKEYONAWAFFLE

Tasks to Try:

Think about and write down your favourite smells, tastes, sounds, touches and sights. Enlighten your senses by seeking out at least one for each sense. It's a meditative method as well as a bit of fun. You could also start a conversation about what other people love – ask them and see their eyes light up with passion.

Your Notes:

· ·

· ·

· ·

· ·

A
B
C

Sex

I couldn't write a calmness, kindness and happiness book without a section about sex, as sex usually has the elements of showing kindness, to bring about happiness, to then feel calm. It's such an important topic that often doesn't get talked about enough. And when it is talked about there are a lot of misconceptions, assumptions and awkwardness!

Across countries and cultures you get vastly different ideas about sex. One thing the human race has in common is that we are hard wired to seek out sex for reproductive purposes. And for the majority of humans, sex causes pleasure. As talked about in the Identity and Uniqueness topics, everyone is different. Different sexualities, preferences and beliefs. It's amazing nowadays, compared to when I grew up, how much things have changed in terms of expression and acceptance, but there's still a long way to go.

The reality of sex I feel needs to be spoken about a lot more. Porn shouldn't be used for education, especially for children and teenagers, because the vast majority is pretty toxic. It doesn't reflect real life bodies or sex. So much of it is extreme and hints at illegal situations. People watching porn to learn about sex is dangerous and damaging. Assuming the average penis size is grotesquely big and thinking vulvas are like a doll's can effect peoples' own body images, as well as their expectations of a sexual partner. People think they need to re-enact what they see - that they should do or should enjoy things when they don't. They also get confused with what is legal and what is OK. The titles of porn videos are shocking and confusing enough, suggesting things like incest, and that's without even watching them. It's generally the case that porn far from reflects equality between sexual partners.

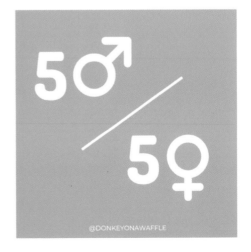

I personally feel that sex should be equal with regards to consent, safety and respect. When going into a relationship, it should be assumed

Sex

that both people have equal roles in giving and receiving pleasure. If an open discussion means both people agree to it not being equal then fine, that is still fair and respectful. Inequality has been rife in history and usually occurred in a heterosexual relationship, with women believed to be the 'lesser' gender. But as you'll see below, it's not just heterosexual women who have had it bad in the past. It's interesting to learn about sex throughout history, here are a few snippets:

Birth control, as well as abortion, goes back as far as 1850 BC in Ancient Egypt.

Homosexuality was very common in ancient Greece and Rome. Women and children were generally the property of the man of the family, but these men would often have a young male lover too. A woman caught committing adultery could be killed by her husband, and a wife who drank more than a moderate amount of wine was grounds for divorce.

There are plenty of literary references to the use of dildos in ancient Greece – they were made of padded leather and anointed with olive oil.

Between 400 and 100 AD, the Christian church deemed masturbation, oral sex, anal sex and homosexuality as punishable. Sex within marriage was tolerated for reproductive purposes only and contraception was banned.

Between 1533 and 1835, England's 'Buggery Act' meant sodomy was punishable by execution.

In the 1800s, female sexual tension was diagnosed as 'hysteria', a nervous condition that could cause insanity.

In Victorian times there was a wild spread of sexually transmitted diseases. In 1839 in London, a city of two million inhabitants, there were estimated to be around 80,000 prostitutes.

The 1960s were revolutionary for women – only married women – as they could get the contraceptive Pill (if their husband agreed). It was only from 1974 that single women could have it prescribed.

Tasks to Try:

Even if you think you know all there is to know, do some research this week on sex. There are some hilarious theories and beliefs throughout history as well as some shocking truths and stats. You might improve your knowledge, your teaching skills for your children and of course, your sex life.

Your Notes:

. . . .

. . . .

A
B
. . . .   C

. . . .

Slow Down

Before covid-19, I would've asked, "When do you last remember doing nothing?" When people were in lockdown, many couldn't work, or were on furlough, or had very little to do as everything was closed and we weren't allowed to go out. So during this time, some people slowed down and loved the slower pace of life without all the pressure and mental load of daily life. Other people were busier than normal, as they were having to work from home and home-school their children at the same time. What most people realised is just how busy modern life is, whether it was the change to slowing down or trying to juggle everything and not having a work / life balance. Overthinking is a huge problem of recent times as we are all so busy. We struggle to process the day so when it comes to going to sleep, our brain gets stuck trying to process everything. Our mental computer can't run its night-time back-up because we have too many files open!

We live in a world of multi-tasking, it's very normal now to be working, talking and listening to something all at the same time. It's also common to assume we've had a productive day if we work late and come home exhausted. The problem is that there will always be more things to do no matter how many jobs you do and how fast you do them. We clutch at the idea of higher efficiency because it helps to maintain the illusion that we can get everything done. But we have to learn to do what matters and tolerate leaving other things undone. Something has to give and that choice is yours: do you settle for an untidy house or not be the employee who always does overtime, so you can spend more time socialising with friends or reading with your children? Consciously making the decision is key, so you're not then worrying or thinking about how messy your house is or doing that overtime. Many people get their sense of self-worth from their work but no one aged 90 will boast of always having an empty inbox in their working life.

The present moment sounds so ordinary

but actually it's incredible - and it's a gift. If you're always racing to the next moment, what happens to the one you're in? The Be Present topic talks about this in more depth.

In general, people slow down either when on holiday or when they're forced to (like in lockdown). Evenings and weekends may be slower than the manic week of work or study but people generally try to cram in as much as they can whether it's seeing people, exercise, chores at home, hobbies etc. It's also the mental and emotional side that we can slow down on. Having an active mind and thinking about all aspects of our life including planning and problems, is exhausting. We can start to think about what we can let go of - physically not doing certain things and mentally what can we think less about. Doing and thinking about more of what we love rather than filling ourselves with so much of what we don't love.

Tasks to Try:

Treat yourself - whether it's painting your nails, having a massage, a haircut, a bath with special salts and candles. Do something or many things you like doing to pamper yourself so that you slow down and have a moment to sit, think and relax.
We try to mark 'lockdown days' in our calendars now, to take us back to the slower pace of life. It means we're less tired and means we spend that quality time together again that was the luxury of lockdown.

Your Notes:

A
B
C

Social Media

Social media is a reflection of our basic human need to relate and fit in. It is great for this in so many ways, in ways like sharing photos, funny articles, celebrating events such as passing exams, birthdays etc. But, it can get to a stage where people are hooked on getting attention and when they don't get it, they feel down. There is pressure to have or do things that others show and post. Western societies are becoming more self-centred, vain and narcissistic. FOMO (Fear of Missing Out) commonly affects all of us. If we stop using social media, we think we'll miss out on important news or updates from our social circles. The likelihood is that if a close friend or family member has important news, they'll contact you directly!

Studies show an association between social media use and anxiety among emerging adults - who are already at high risk of anxiety disorders. Sadly, people who spend a lot of time on social media sites report feeling lonely and isolated in real life. You can boost your mood by simply going out in public, seeing friends or going to your favourite park or cafe. When you do go on social media, make sure your feed is balanced. Only follow people who make you feel good or have a positive message.

People do not act on social media as they would in person, so you may get a distorted interaction from anyone you communicate with. This could be a more abrupt reply from a friend, to the more dangerous anonymous trolling, catfishing, bullying etc. Deleting and unfollowing negative accounts or people is vital.

Don't let social media drag you where you don't want to go

I studied Biology at University and one thing that stuck out when learning about human behaviour and connections was 'Dunbar's number'. We can keep between 100-250 (most commonly quoted as 150) meaningful, stable, social relationships with other people - ones in which we know that person relatively well and are in social contact with them regularly. Robin Dunbar explained it informally as "the number of people you wouldn't feel embarrassed about joining uninvited for a drink if you happened to bump into them in a bar". Looking at evolution, when humans started to use language, the ability to communicate with people within a social group, went from one to one grooming, to talking in multiple groups. This allowed early humans to maintain social cohesion more efficiently and social groups, tribes or communities could therefore grow over time. One person talking usually means up to three people are listening. You may notice that when a group becomes five or more, it usually splits so two or more people are talking. Throughout history and various cultures, 150 is most often the number within historical settlements and farming villages, in tribal communities past and present, and in social media. It's the average and ultimate number of 'genuine' friends we have, not just acquaintances, that really counts. Nowadays, compared to times before social media, we can be over-connected to too many people, platforms, across too many countries and continents. If it feels overwhelming it's because humans aren't built for all these connections.

The various platforms we use can be more of a distraction than a connection, a habit rather than have any purpose. A statistic from 2017 stated that people in their 20s and 30s check social media an average 157 times a day. Getting a notification on our phones activates our dopamine system - we literally get a small hit of the feel good hormone as it's validating our need for attention and excitement. Dopamine doesn't result in long term happiness though, not like serotonin and oxytocin do. These two hormones come from feelings of contentment, security and warm love... not the love button on Facebook or Instagram!

The benefits of detoxing from social media include improving your overall mood and mental health, reconnecting with the real world, freeing up time to do more of the things you love and conquering FOMO.

Tasks to Try:

Give yourself a time of day to use social media. So instead of checking your phone however many times a day, (usually scrolling aimlessly), just check in blocks so it limits your time - when you decide to. You can give yourself a goal e.g. to cut your social media time in half or to stop at a certain time in the evening. Other ideas are to designate a phone-free zone or room where you live, limit your number of posts per week, turn off notifications or even turn your phone settings to greyscale so social media is much less compelling! You could also delete an app - just for 1 week, then see if you missed it or missed out.

If you love social media for your own memories and photos, create a private account. It may be liberating to post photos without the pressure of looking your best, but have them for your own pleasure of looking back at your year. See how it feels to be the curator of what you want to see rather than how others see your life.

Your Notes:

. . . .

. . . .

. . . .

. . . .

A
B
C

Stuff

It's a fair assumption that most of us have too much stuff and / or we buy unnecessary stuff for others. When it comes to birthdays and Christmas there's a social pressure to buy more and more things for more and more people. There's also an age old joke that come January, everyone's got a pile of unwanted gifts.

In America on Black Friday, sale volumes go up by 1500% - shoppers in 2018 spent more than $717billion. Then there are the fights, arguments and crazy queuing - all over the desperation to buy stuff, most of which ends up in landfill within a year.

Canada started a "Buy Nothing Day" in 1992 which is now in 65 countries around the world, including the UK. It's always on a Friday at the end of November and is a way to "escape the shopocalypse" of Black Friday!

It's not just about shopping and buying stuff. Greenpeace UK's Oceans Campaigner said "Even free stuff has a price, and our oceans, forests and wildlife are paying their share of that price, even when you aren't."

The fashion industry is one of the world's most polluting industries - it's responsible for more greenhouse gas emissions than shipping and flying combined! This is due to a huge acceleration in fast fashion. When I was a teenager, I had mostly hand-me-downs from my sister, there was little pressure to be "in fashion", shopping for clothes was a rare treat, nothing was online and I wore everything until it was worn out. It seems to have flipped to the polar opposite over the last two decades. Every 5 minutes, 1 million pieces of clothing are made and more than half are thrown away within a year. Raw materials are a massive strain on the planet, they take a ton of water and pesticide to produce. E.g., one pair of jeans takes 8,000 litres to make. Then there's the transport, packaging

Want less, Live more

@DONKEYONAWAFFLE

Stuff

etc and the fact so much gets discarded into landfills. My friend introduced me to the book 'Stuffocation' by James Wallman which says: "Having everything we thought we wanted isn't making us happier. It's bad for the planet. It's cluttering up our homes. It's making us feel 'stuffocated' and stressed"

The book explores our desires for buying caused by advertising, the link between materialism and declining well-being, and the trend in 'experientialism' – which is about finding happiness and meaning (and even expressing status) through experiences rather than being obsessed with stuff.

I've always preferred spending money on experiences, so doing things and going places, rather than having objects. The pursuit of buying an object rarely keeps the same buzz, charm or excitement once it's bought. The novelty wears off and people look for what to buy next. Instead of looking to buy new things or change the things around you, focus on yourself and what you may want to do instead of what you may want to have.

"Too many people spend money they haven't earned, to buy things they don't want, to impress people they don't like" – Will Rogers

The best things in life

...are free

- Luther Vandross

@DONKEYONAWAFFLE

Tasks to Try:

When you're wanting to buy something, ask yourself "do I really need it?" Think about a few things you've bought recently and how long the good feeling lasted, and whether you still use those things? When you need an item, can you buy second-hand, borrow or rent / hire?

With your wardrobe, can you do a clothes swap with friends? Can you get any clothes altered, repaired or jazz them up somehow?

If you get too much stuff you don't need given to you as presents, start asking people not to get you things, or suggest to do something with that person instead of buying each other gifts.

Ask yourself when have you felt happiest? When have you been most calm? Are they moments you've had that haven't costed anything, e.g., with loved ones, at home or in nature? Most peoples' happiest and calmest times aren't buying material things, they're doing and being. Think of these times when you're feeling the need to spend when you know you shouldn't.

Your Notes:

Touch

Touch is a sense that we probably used to take for granted, but since covid-19, we may have realised how important it is. From all the family and friends we long or longed to hug, to simply being tactile with people, whether it's sitting next to them or touching on the arm while chatting away. Research is suggesting that touch is truly fundamental to human communication, bonding and health in the following ways:

Pain - Touching someone you love can reduce physical pain.

Security - When we're touched in a comfortable way, our neurological senses are ignited through the skin, and our brain gets the emotional response that we're feeling safe, secure and good.

Calm - If you've had an overwhelming day, a good hug can do wonders to help you relax. It reduces cortisol and increases oxytocin. Which leads onto....

Health - When you're feeling reassured with touch, your blood pressure and pulse decrease as you are calming your body, which puts less stress on your heart. These physical benefits of hugging and touch can lead to a healthier, longer life. Every time you lower your cortisol, this has an impact on your immune system so you're increasing your ability to fight disease.

Hugging is a beautiful form of touch communication that lets a person know that they matter. We express various kinds of emotions through hugs, including happiness, excitement, fear, sadness, pity, love, comfort, protection, grief and admiration. There's a deep human connection that comes from linking your body with another person's and momentarily linking your souls. Imagine you lost your sense of touch altogether and got it back after years, how amazing things would feel, not just

Touch comes before sight,
before speech
It is the first language,
and the last

@DONKEYONAWAFFLE

people but objects and animals too. However, it is crucial to always remember that hugs and touch must be agreed to by both parties. Touching someone who doesn't want to be, is extremely disrespectful and can cause physical or mental damage. Some people aren't tactile, some are very private, and some have issues with touch. Forcing hugs is a huge no-no in my eyes, especially with children. It's totally wrong to say they should hug someone to say hello, goodbye or thank you. Their body is theirs and they can choose. Just as your body is yours and you make your own choices.

There are some people who prefer animal hugs to human hugs and these can be just as beneficial. In a study of patients who'd had heart attacks, the chances of them dying within a year was 400% less if they owned a dog. The assumption was that this result was due to the exercise of walking a dog, but a significant effect comes from the owner–dog relationship. Interacting warmly with your dog for 30 minutes can increase oxytocin levels by 300% (and by 130% in your dog).

A pet's cortisol levels can also decrease when being stroked or cuddled. And our cortisol levels can also decrease (unless you don't like animals of course). Stroke therapy is becoming more popular in hospitals, where stroking a therapy dog (or the patient's own dog) helps to calm the patient, make them feel good and this aids recovery. I've even seen a therapy pony in a hospital!

The effect of animals is also well-known in areas such as autism. Animal-assisted therapy is considered to be a valuable addition to treatment possibilities for reducing stress and improving social communication in people with autism spectrum disorder. Research shows that children with autism experience fewer meltdowns in the presence of a pet dog that they interact with.

A hug can be worth more than a thousand words

AVO-CUDDLE

@DONKEYONAWAFFLE

Tasks to Try:

If you hug friends or family when you meet, give extra good hugs. Like you really mean it, but only if the other person is willing and not so long that it's awkward!

Think about the feeling of touch and what textures you love. Stroke a friend's cat, ask a stranger with a dog to say hello, feel a silk piece of clothing through your hands or on your face. Feel the rain. Wrap up warm and intentionally go out when it's cold. Coming back into the cosy warmth, feeling that contrast is revitalising, refreshing, and you appreciate having a home.

Your Notes:

A
B
C

Travel

When the covid-19 pandemic hit, we all either stopped or heavily limited travel. Since this happened, people may now think differently about travel, like how it's better for the planet when we travel less and how much more we can discover in our local area. Most of us probably struggle with not being able to travel, as humans naturally want to move, socialise and explore. But we can adapt, and adopt a "holiday attitude" at home. When some of us stay at home and do less, this is reflective of what most of us do when we travel – we slow down, spend time outside and explore new things to do.

Children have the ability to view the world as constant exploration, stumbling across one wonder to the next in curiosity and awe. And this can be in your garden or local park. Being an explorer is a state of mind. Travel doesn't have to be far at all. To some, travel means adventure, escape, peace and new experiences. To others it's simply about spending quality time with family or friends. Ultimately, we travel in search of a feeling and we receive all these benefits in return:

Boosting our immunity: Apart from with viral diseases when they don't have a cure, in other circumstances, when we're somewhere different, our bodies are exposed to new kinds of bacteria and produce antibodies, which protect us from potential future illnesses.

Strengthening our relationships: As we try new things and share experiences with someone, we form bonds and memories with that person. Couples who travel together generally have better communication – apart from those moments of getting lost!

Improving bone health: Generally, we spend more time outside when we travel. When our skin is exposed to sunlight, the ultraviolet B (UVB) rays hit cholesterol in the skin cells, providing the energy for vitamin D synthesis to occur. Vitamin D helps us absorb

Once a year, go someplace you've never been before

- DALAI LAMA

@DONKEYONAWAFFLE

Travel

calcium from our food into our bones, so strengthening our bones and protecting us from osteoporosis. Opportunities for self-reflection, new perspectives and clarity:

Exploring new places, meeting new people and learning about different cultures makes us more open-minded, trusting, empathetic and tolerant. When we travel, we're put into unfamiliar situations, and interact with strangers, especially if we're travelling alone. This can improve our confidence and our sense of self.

Encouraging less materialism: I personally value experiences over buying and owning a product, as you can't put a price on funny, warming or happy memories. It's even been labelled a recent trend to reject material possessions and aspire to have nothing. And I believe this makes us more grateful and less stressed.

Improving physical and mental health by decreasing stress and depression: The things we tend to do on holiday are usually mood enhancers, from getting more sleep and exercise, to meeting new people and creating happy memories. Sunlight, exercise and positive experiences all increase our serotonin levels. Even planning a holiday can result in feeling happier. Travelling also reduces stress by removing us from the pressures of everyday life and work. We're distracted from our daily issues and commitments, so we experience less anxiety.

We travel not to escape life

But for life not to escape us

@DONKEYONAWAFFLE

Tasks to Try:

Research your local area, ask around for new places to discover. You can travel on your own doorstep and still get the same benefits of travelling far. If you can and want to travel further, look into a few places, take time to research where you'd like to explore. My dad and his friends go on holiday together every year. To decide where to go next they have a get together and everyone pitches an idea of a place they've researched and why they want to go there. Then they vote!

Your Notes:

· ·

· ·

A

B

· ·

C

· ·

Uniqueness

Everyone is unique and our traits change with age, others' influence and life events. Personality tests and categories can be subjective but they can enlighten us in learning about ourselves and about others. Seeing the world through someone else's eyes can help in work, conflict - and love. It's so easy to assume people think like us but in reality, no one thinks exactly the same as us. Exploring traits and seeing them as scales rather than black and white (and never right or wrong) can be interesting. Here are some examples:

Extroverts and introverts: These always seem polar opposites so you're one or the other, but there is still a scale, plus you can be an antisocial extrovert or a sociable introvert like me. Extroverts thrive and get their energy from interacting with others as they focus outwards, into the world. Introverts need to recharge on our own as we focus inward, into our own thoughts.

Inner and outer expectations: People find it either easy or hard to meet their own expectations, such as keeping motivated to reach the goals we aim for, the resolutions we make or the deadlines we set. So that is one part. We then also find it either easy or hard to meet external expectations, which is about what others expect of us, whether it's letting people down, questioning or sticking to rules or making commitments to others. If like me, you readily meet outer expectations, but resist meeting inner expectations, it may be that you wouldn't miss a work deadline, but find it hard to exercise on your own. Knowing this, can help for planning ahead. If you know you're going to find something difficult as it's "just for you", it could be a good idea to create outer accountability. E.g., exercising with a friend or having a weekly check-in text with someone about continuing a resolution.

Don't be afraid of being different. Be afraid of being the same as everyone else

@DONKEYONAWAFFLE

Detail vs bigger picture: Detail people tend to be conscientious and exacting, but can lack perspective or fail to prioritise. Big picture people tend to be creative and visionary, but they can be disorganized and forgetful. This doesn't sound like a huge issue, but it can really help with work colleagues if you know what their preference is. It can save you time writing out huge detail in an email to someone who just wants a summary. Or it can keep you from thinking someone's acting abruptly or being dismissive - a short email doesn't mean they don't like or respect you, it's just their way.

'Submodalities' or 'representational systems': These reflect a set of preferences that you use to think and express yourself. People can use all ways of expression, but usually have a dominant method out of: visual, audio, kinaesthetic or audio digital. Visual is if you can imagine a picture well and may say "I see what you mean". Audio is if you respond to sound, music, volume, tone and may say "I hear what you're saying". Kinaesthetic is if you have intuitions and may say "I feel a hint of..." Audio digital is if you have an internal dialogue and you like processes, so you may say "I think I understand". One example is when someone gives you directions, a visual preference likes to see or draw a map whereas an audio preference can remember the instructions they hear.

Look back to the Be Present topic for in-time and through-time tendencies.

Tasks to Try:

Take some quizzes or tests - even if you've done one before, the results may come out differently, or try one you've not seen before. You may learn something about yourself. You can also think of someone close to you or someone who you've had differences with and try to understand their perspective - most people have good intentions so it can be just a difference in tendencies.
Think up some of your own questions, ask and answer them as a game with a friend or family member - you'll learn about yourself and them and vice versa.

Your Notes:

Values

Passion could be a separate topic in itself but it's so linked to values that it's useful to talk about them together. Passion is an internal motivator, an energy enabling you to follow your values. Our values keep passion moving in a productive path towards fulfilling our purpose.

Tim Minchin did an amazing and passionate speech called "Live To Learn". He talked about the fact that sometimes people have a tendency to define themselves in opposition to things, talking about things they disagree with or dislike. Expressing your passion for things you love is so much more pleasant to hear. "Be pro-stuff, not just anti-stuff."

There's a French phrase that captures the expression of joy and the cheerful, passionate lust for life. 'Joie de Vivre' is using your five senses to explore, breathe, laugh, appreciate and enjoy what surrounds you. It's a drive to have the life you desire and it's the connection with your spirit, your values and your passions.

There's an idealistic phrase that people should "Do what they love and love what they do". Some people are lucky enough to turn their passions into their careers, but most people, around 80%, don't love their jobs. And we spend more than a third of our lives at work – 90,000 hours! It's easy to get whisked away into a world of work, home, eat, sleep, repeat... and forgetting about our values and what we'd really like to do. Two questions to ask are:

1) What makes you happy?

2) If you had all the time and money in the world, what would you do?

Thinking about your values and beliefs is about being the best version of yourself you can be. This kind of personal development can bring up some thought provoking questions and may

help with any problems you face. You can become clear on who you are, what you want your life to stand for, and where you want to go in life. This clarity will increase your sense of control which elevates happiness levels. Another important question to ask yourself is this:

What is truly important to you in life? Knowing this makes decision making easier as you can align your decisions with your values.

A friend told me about an expert in values called Steve Pavlina. He demonstrates that it's crucial to note that you don't have to live by the same values all your life. You can consciously change them, e.g., you can go from someone who values peace the most, to someone whose top priority is success. Paths in life change so you can re-visit your values as many times as you wish. When you change your values list and consciously act on them, you change your behaviour and therefore your results. And this can lead to incredible new experiences (see the Comfort Zone topic and Habits and Goals topic). So how can you decide how to make changes in your life?

There are two ways, you can derive your goals from your values or derive your values from your goals. So you'll have two lists - values and goals, each in order of priority at this time of your life. I personally prefer Steve Pavlina's method of deciding on goals first, which are your destinations you want to reach, and then values can be adapted to fit those goals. Then when a goal is reached, a new values list can be created. The tasks go into this in more detail.

When your values are clear to you, making decisions becomes easier

@DONKEYONAWAFFLE

Tasks to Try:

Make a list of goals. Examples may be to improve your health or fitness, learn a new skill, move house, climb a mountain, travel, give a talk in public, run a marathon, redecorate... Work out which ones are most important to you and prioritise them.

Next write down 10 values that are most important to you. Examples are: happiness, kindness, calmness, learning, love, health, wealth, fun, passion, security, discipline, integrity, achievement, creativity and humility. Then put your list into order of priority as well. One way to decide the priorities is ask yourself "If I could only satisfy one of these values, which would it be?" This is your top priority. Then you can go down your list and think about each one separately and compare that value to every other word and decide which is more important to you. E.g., if you have Respect, Adventure, Independence and Humour, think which is more important: Respect vs Adventure, Respect vs Independence and Respect vs Humour. This may take some thought so take your time and come back to it a few times.

Next step is to see whether your values and goals lists fit together. Is there anything you may change to align them? E.g., if family, health and fun are top of your values list and getting a promotion is top of your goals list, this may make you stop and think. E.g., if travelling around the world is your top goal, and wealth and comfort are bottom of your values list with adventure at the top, this is aligned. You can use these lists to help make decisions, realise what's most important to you and who you want to be.

Your Notes:

• •

• •

A
B
C

• •

• •

Visual

Sight is arguably our most important sense in day to day life. Most of us can imagine pictures in our minds. This is why visualisations can be a powerful tool for coping with emotions.

My daughters, like many children and adults alike, suffer from nightmares. They used to be so bad they'd wake crying through the night, we'd all bed swap and lose a lot of sleep. Nightmares can hit all the senses but they're mainly visual. There was a recurring nightmare about a green witch that was particularly troublesome to my 6 year old. So at bedtime I'd get her to pretend to take the image out of her head, put it on my hand and describe it in her own words. I'd then tell her to imagine the image getting smaller, quieter, further away and to the side of her vision (so not directly in front of her). The green witch would fade into the corner of her room and what's important is that she would be doing the visualisation. So that if the witch appeared in a dream, she had the power to fade her away again. Having had months of nightmares, she suddenly had none after doing this technique. There is the odd one now and again but we repeat or change the exercise slightly. Sometimes it'd be a case of her conjuring up a pet dragon who stomps on the witch to squash her... that worked too!

Visualisations can be just as powerful in adults. If you're in a horrible situation where you feel stressed, anxious, afraid or awkward, you can visualise something that takes you to a better state. People have a 'happy place' and imagine themselves on a clear, crisp mountain top, or on a beach with a cocktail, or in an autumnal forest with beautiful colours all around. That alone can calm and distract. Or visualising the end of the horrible situation, so imagining where you will be afterwards whether it's in an hour or a month. Thinking about the reality that it will end or change is useful, healthy and stops the feelings of stress from getting out of control.

What we see depends mainly on what we look for

@DONKEYONAWAFFLE

It's mentioned in the Habits and Goals

topic, but visualising every aspect of a goal in detail can help you reach that goal. It also brings about positive vibes which motivates you to act on the goal.

The other side of sight is what we see around us, which is touched on in the Senses topic, but includes the much talked about screen time. Most of us watch too much TV or are exposed to too much screen time. However, it can be a great method of winding down, zoning out and relaxing. If you're watching a screen anyway, you can think more consciously about how you use that time. Whether it's watching something totally new that you wouldn't normally try, something educational instead of programmes that are 'easy' or something really old that you've not seen in years to evoke feelings of nostalgia. Laughing or remembering something fondly can set off the feel good hormones in your body like dopamine.

Tasks to Try:

Look deeper at the world around you. Imagine you're entering a photo competition so you look at things for longer and appreciate the beauty of the colours, shadows, textures and shapes. Take a mental snapshot of a happy place so you can visualise this easier when you need to feel calmer or happier. Even better, draw your happy place or have a photo of it in your home.

Think of some nostalgic films, from your childhood, or teenage years. Look up a new comedy or educational program. Find something you're in the mood for and have a good reminisce or belly laugh.

Your Notes:

· ·

· ·

· ·

· ·

A
B
C

Warm Words of the World

Words can be so powerful and sometimes they're simply fun. There are about 6,500 languages around the world and so many have single words to describe situations or feelings that take a whole sentence to explain in English! This is a section of beautiful words which evoke humour and happiness:

Ahimsa - Sanskrit word which means non-violence. It embodies respect, patience and compassion for all things. Approaching things softly, speaking in a receptive voice, slowing down.

Akihi (Hawaiian): Listening to directions and then walking off and promptly forgetting them!

Basorexia (English): A sudden and overwhelming urge or hunger to kiss someone!

Coddiwomple: An old English slang word meaning to travel purposefully towards an as-yet-unknown destination.

Commuovere (Italian): To be moved in a heart-warming way, usually related to a story that moved you to tears.

Fika (Swedish): A moment to slow down to appreciate the good things in life, like coffee with a friend.

Firgun (Hebrew): Genuine, unselfish delight or pride in the accomplishment of another.

Flibbertigibbet (English). Referring to someone who is silly and who talks incessantly. The first known usage of this word is the 15th century and used to be spelled flepergebet. This word also refers to a person who is flighty.

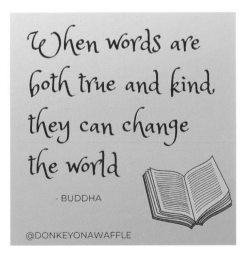

When words are both true and kind, they can change the world

- BUDDHA

@DONKEYONAWAFFLE

Warm Words of the World

Gezelligheid (Dutch): Sharing someone's company with a pleasant, friendly ambience. Having an upbeat feeling about the cosy surroundings.

Hwyl (Welsh): A stirring feeling of emotional motivation and energy. High spirits.

Hygge (Danish): Enjoying life's simple pleasures: Friends. Family. Graciousness. A form of everyday togetherness.

Ikigai (Japanese): A reason for being; encompassing joy, a sense of purpose and meaning and a feeling of well-being.

Lagom (Swedish): Balanced, enough, sufficient, adequate, just right.

Liming (Trinidad & Tobago) - Referring to the art of doing nothing while sharing food, drink, conversation and laughter, liming is an important part of the country's island culture. In fact, it's not uncommon for locals to say something like "let's go lime" to mean "let's chill or hangout."

Mamihlapinatapei (Yagan - Indigenous language of the Tierra del Fuego region in South America) - A meaningful look between two people - both wanting to initiate something but reluctant to begin.

Retrouvailles (French): Refindings. Referring to the reunion you have with someone you care deeply for but whom you have not seen in a long time.

Scurryfunge (commonly used in 19th Century England) - A hasty tidying of the house when a last minute guest in coming.

Sisu (Finnish): Roughly translated into English as strength of will, determination, perseverance, and acting rationally in the face of adversity. Gutsy would be the closest word. It symbolises courage & resilience. It is said to boost your well-being, support you to reach your goals & help you to fight fairly, with honesty & humility.

Sobremesa (Spanish) - Sharing food & conservation with loved ones. The sobremesa is a Spanish tradition that involves spending time relaxing after a meal to drink coffee or digestive liquor or to just continue hanging out chatting at the table after eating.

Ukiyo (Japanese): Living in the moment, detached from the bothers of life – also described as the 'The Floating World'

Xertz. When you're outside in the summer heat doing something active, making you thirsty. When you then drink an ice cold glass of water (or drink of your choice!) and gulp it down quickly or greedily, helping to quench your thirst and cool yourself down. When you do this, it is called xertz.

Tasks to Try:

See if you can apply as much of this list as possible in your life this week. Name the positive feeling or situation, say it out loud or tell another person who is there. It's a special thing to teach someone something new or inspire them. Plus you're both more likely to feel and remember that moment.

Your Notes:

A
B
C

Write

Not everyone wants to or can talk about their feelings with a partner, friend or therapist. However you can listen to yourself by writing your thoughts down. Being aware of your emotions can be very liberating and once they're written down, they won't be whizzing round your head as much. Writing is self-therapy, escapism, relief and encourages creativity, clarity, calmness and empathy.

Another reason to write or keep a journal is that it can accelerate your ability to manifest your goals. As you read and re-write your goals daily, they'll become forged into your subconscious mind. Eventually, your dreams and vision will consume your inner world and can quickly become your physical reality.

A friend introduced me to Julia Cameron's 'morning pages' idea where you write for three pages - consciously, longhand and not typing. This slows you down which helps connect you to your emotions. There's no wrong way but the aim is to write out anything and everything that crosses your mind, for your eyes only. By carrying out this practice, people have come up with ideas that have changed their work or social life, understood and worked through issues, felt more in tune with their intuition, and it's shown them what to prioritise, what to focus on or what situations to leave.

When one area of our life takes over or isn't given enough attention, it's common to feel like something is missing. The core elements that make up our lives are generally thought to be: Family, Work, Friends, Well-being, Relationship, Adventure, Money and Home. We need to balance our time and efforts amongst them. Some parts you may neglect, some parts you may feel stuck and other parts you may not realise how important they are to you (see the Values topic).

Writing is exploration. You start from nothing and learn as you go

@DONKEYONAWAFFLE

Taking time to think and write about the different areas of your life can bring certain aspects to the forefront of your mind. It's a great thing to consider all these parts of your life and to question yourself. Thinking about what you want to be remembered for and writing a few sentences down can give you a deeper purpose to your life. Looking at your written paragraph daily means you'll connect your daily actions with your legacy. Knowing and living your values will lead to a sense of balance, confidence and fulfilment. And any regret will be diminished.

Tasks to Try:

Write how you feel each day this week. You could write a diary, adopt the morning pages habit or just jot down a few feelings you have and why. Try writing in a colour pen so different to the normal blue or black used for work, lists etc. If you have a block, try drawing or doodling as this can help open up thoughts. Or try the following suggestions.

Draw a circle with 8 segments (like a pizza). Each segment represents Family, Work, Friends, Well-being, Relationship, Adventure, Money and Home. Colour each segment according to how happy you are with that part of your life, so 1/10 would be awful and near the centre of the circle and 10/10 would be the whole segment coloured in. For each segment, start to think about how you could improve it by 1 point by doing something small, then by 3 points over the coming months by changing something bigger. (See Motivation topic and Habits and Goals topic).

Question yourself – for fun, imagination or to find more meaning:

1) How would you describe yourself in 5 words?

2) Whose opinion matters to you the most?

3) How would that person or your best friend or family member describe you?

4) Would they use the same words as you gave yourself?

5) What are your unique selling points? (Imagine you are a brand)

6) What do people thank you for?

7) If you have just one role to fulfil on this earth, what is it?

8) What matters to you and why?

9) What would your 9 year old self tell you now?

10) What would your 90 year old self tell you now?

11) What do you love doing the most?

12) What can you give yourself more credit for?

13) What's the biggest obstacle standing in your way and what can you do to move past it?

Your Notes:

• •

• •

• •

• •

A
B
C

Your Tribe

As human beings we mostly need to belong to a social group or tribe. This social group could be our family, community or friendship group, and can be at home, school or at work. We all need to feel we belong and are valued. This is talked about in the Community and Childhood topics.

This section is about finding your type of person who you click with. This usually means sharing the same values, opinions and outlook on life. When you start a new class or hobby, or volunteer for a charity you're passionate about, or go to a festival with music you love, or start a new job you have a huge interest in, or join a sports event... you'll be surrounded by like-minded people doing and enjoying the same thing. Even meeting someone in an everyday situation can spark things in common and it's a great feeling when you have this rapport with someone. It's so easy to go through life spending time with people who are nice and who you have social connections with, but make sure you have time for the people who you really want to spend time with. See more of who makes you feel special, see more of who you love, see more of who you click with. A friend read me a poem by Susanna Michaelis which said, "Kindle the kind of friendship you dream about – soul friends are the greatest treasure".

Psychosocial stress is when you don't know how to interpret the intention or behaviour of others, and this stress has been shown to be stronger than a physical attack in terms of the release of cortisol in your body. Being with people you're not that comfortable with or who you just don't get, can be incredibly stressful. So find the people who you do get - and who get you!

Being aware of who you ask advice from is important and your tribe could be a good place to start. Sadly, some people may feel threatened by you and they could minimise your idea

Don't chase people, or change so people will like you.
Be yourself and the right people will love you.

@DONKEYONAWAFFLE

or be critical in some way. You need someone to be honest and real, but you also need someone who wants you to succeed so will motivate you. With anything in life, people have hugely varying opinions. If you need advice about a subject, ask a few people you trust and then decide yourself with the information you have.

Tasks to Try:

Follow your tribe – think about who you click with and whether you'd like to or can spend more time with them. Next time you meet someone who you click with, have the confidence to invite them to something whether it's a coffee or an event. Search for groups in your area that do activities you're passionate about, because finding like-minded souls reignites or keeps a passion aflame!

I was part of a meditation group and one challenge we did which can be really therapeutic, is to think about and write down all the people who you trust, rely on and who have inspired you in any aspect of your life. Who is your tribe, past and present? What qualities do they have and what effect have they had on your life? Anyone who has influenced you or contributed to your growth and development. When working through your list, think carefully about why you chose each person. What has changed in your life for the better? You can adapt this in your own way by choosing people who have negative qualities, but who you learned from because of this. You may even want to include celebrities, writers and personalities who you don't know personally but who have still influenced you. It may be 10 people, it may be 100, depending how detailed you want to go.

Your Notes:

· ·

· ·

A
B
C

· ·

· ·

There are three main reasons why we sleep – restoration, energy conservation and brain function. There are some genes that are only switched on when we sleep and these are to do with resting and healing. In order to restore, replace and rebuild within our bodies, we need to sleep. The brain function part is to do with us learning and processing the day. Studies show that sleep helps with learning tasks and insightful behaviour. So when we sleep, we remember information more easily and also gain insight to solve existing problems. When we sleep, the hippocampus sorts and stores the memories it's received during the day.

Sleep deprivation shuts down this memory inbox so it can't commit learning to memory. As well as poor memory, lack of sleep leads to poor judgement and increased impulsiveness. It also affects our immunity as it switches off genes that are associated with our immune system. When we're deprived of sleep, we then tend to use stimulants like caffeine to feel more awake in the day and alcohol in the evening to wind down. Alcohol is a sedative but it only mimics sleep, and harms the processes of memory consolidation and recall that occur during proper sleep.

Tiredness is associated with two hormones which do opposite jobs. Leptin suppresses hunger and ghrelin – known as the 'hunger hormone' – increases hunger. They are both involved in the regulation of appetite, metabolism, fat storage and calorie burning. Lack of sleep leads to an increase of ghrelin and a decrease in leptin, resulting in hunger and a general slow-down of metabolism. Both these hormone changes mean weight gain may occur. Tiredness is also associated with stress which in itself leads to suppressed immunity and raised blood pressure.

Sleep is the best meditation

– Dalai Lama

@DONKEYONAWAFFLE

It's recommended that adults should get an average of 8 hours sleep a night (some need more, some need less), but it seems the average length that peopleget is about 6.5 hours. Teenagers need more, around 9 hours, and their body rhythms are different, so they have a biological predisposition to go to bed later and get up later. Circadian rhythms are variations in physiology and behaviour that recur every 24-hours, such as the sleep-wake cycle and daily patterns of hormone release. A study of over 91,000 people showed that disrupted circadian rhythms (i.e. sleep patterns), is associated with low mood disorders, low ratings of happiness and low health satisfaction. The researchers advise turning off all electronic devices before 10pm.

Other tips from experts include being consistent in your timings, as this anchors your sleep and improves the quality. Our bodies need to drop a few degrees to initiate and stay asleep, so they say 18 degrees is optimal for most people. Caffeine is a well-known culprit behind bad sleep. You may think you need caffeine first thing in the morning but your body actually will wake up if you give it more time, with daylight. Caffeine can become a habit and you become reliant on it, but if you try without or at least limit it, after a few days of not feeling so good, you may be able to reduce your intake - if you want to.

When you can't sleep at night, it's because you're awake in someone else's dreams

@DONKEYONAWAFFLE

Tasks to Try:

If you struggle with sleep or feel tired a lot of the time, you could look at your routine and see if anything can change. Examples are:

Make your bedroom a sleep haven by making it as dark as possible.
Don't use your phone for an hour before you go to bed.
Avoid eating an hour before bed.
Go to bed earlier and get up earlier - even by half an hour.
Drink a glass of water when you wake up.
Look at your caffeine intake - can you wait an hour before having your normal coffee in the morning? Can you make the last caffeine intake of the day earlier so it's not so close to bedtime?
Avoid too much alcohol.
Avoid naps during the day.
Be consistent with your bedtime and wake up times.
Keep your bedroom cool.

Your Notes:

A
B
C

Further Reading Ideas and References

ART

TED Talk by Melissa Walker "Art can heal PTSD's invisible wounds"

Aguilar BA. J Pediatr Nurs. 2017 Sep – Oct;36:173-178. The Efficacy of Art Therapy in Pediatric Oncology Patients: An Integrative Literature Review.

BE PRESENT

Hardwiring Happiness: The New Brain Science of Contentment, Calm and Confidence by Rick Hanson

Change Your Life with NLP: the powerful way to make your whole life better by Lindsey Agness

CHILDHOOD

Positive Parenting Solutions – Amy McCready

Big Life Journal – Alexandra

COLOUR

Bourncreative.com

COMFORT ZONE

Intuitivegiraffe.com

P Nixon's stress response curve 1979

Karmakar, R. Psychol Behav Sci Int J. Volume 3 Issue 2 – April 2017. Guidelines for Stress Management

COMMUNITY

Understanding Social Lives: Volume 2 – Open University

COMPLIMENTS

Get Happy by Dr Anthony Gunn

DAYDREAM

To The Lighthouse by Virginia Woolf

Poerio GL et al. Cogn Emot. 2016 Sep;30(6):1197-207. Helping the heart grow fonder during absence: Daydreaming about significant others replenishes connectedness after induced loneliness.

Christine Dell'Amore 2013. Five Surprising Facts About Daydreaming. New computer model aims to simulate our mental escapes. National Geographic

Benjamin Baird et al. Psychological Science Aug 2012. Inspired by Distraction: Mind Wandering Facilitates Creative Incubation

Delaney, P. F., Sahakyan, L., Kelley, C. M., & Zimmerman, C. A. (2010). Remembering to forget: The amnesic effect of daydreaming. Psychological Science, 21(7), 1036-1042

Ellamil, M., Dobson, C., Beeman, M., & Christoff, K. (2012). Evaluative and generative modes of thought during the creative process. Neuroimage, 59(2), 1783-1794

Mar, R. A., Mason, M. F., & Litvack, A. (2012). How daydreaming relates to life satisfaction, loneliness, and social support: The importance of gender and daydream content. Consciousness And Cognition: An International Journal, 21(1), 401-407

Takeuchi, H., Taki, Y., Hashizume, H., Sassa, Y., Nagase, T., Nouchi, R., & Kawashima, R. (2011). Failing to deactivate: The association between brain activity during a working memory task and creativity. Neuroimage, 55(2), 681-687

DECISION MAKING

TED Talk by David Asch - Why it's so hard to make healthy decisions

TED Talk by Dan Gilbert - Why we make bad decisions

Rogers T et al. Commitment Devices: Using Initiatives to Change Behavior. 28th April 2014. American Medical Association.

DECLUTTER

Elinor Ochs, Tamar Kremer-Sadlik, 2013. Fast-Forward Family: Home, Work, and Relationships in Middle-Class America

EMOTIONS

Never Split the Difference by Chris Voss and Tahl Raz

Routledge C et al. Memory. 2012 Jul;20(5):452-60. The power of the past: nostalgia as a meaning-making resource.

TED Talk by Tiffany Watt Smith "The history of human emotions"

TED Talk by Karen Thompson Walker "What fear can teach us"

Ollie and His Super Powers - Ali Knowles

The 7 Habits of Highly Effective People by Steven Covey

ENVIRONMENT

Everyoneofus.co.uk

FOOD

Mujcic R & J Oswald A. Am J Public Health. 2016 Aug;106(8):1504-10. Evolution of Well-Being and Happiness After Increases in Consumption of Fruit and Vegetables.

GRATITUDE

TED Talk by David Steindl-Rast - Want to be happy? Be grateful

Kumar A et al. Undervaluing gratitude: Expressers Misunderstand the Consequences of showing Appreciation Psychol Sci. 2018 Sep;29(9):1423-1435

HABITS and GOALS

TED Talk by Judson Brewer - A simple way to break a bad habit

TED Talk by Srikumar Rao - Plug into your hard-wired happiness

HEALING
On Grief and Grieving by Elizabeth Ross and David Kesler
IDENTITY
Understanding Social Lives: Volume 2 – Open University
JUDGEMENT
New Scientist 28 Sept 2016: We accurately weigh up a person's character in 0.1 seconds by Simon Makin
KINDNESS
Raposa, E et al. Prosocial Behaviour mitigates the negative effects of stress in everyday life. Clin Psy Sci 2016
Deng V et al. Oxytocin modulates proliferation of stress responses of human skin cells. Exp. Derm 2013
McClelland D et al, Psychology and health 1988
The Five Side Effects of Kindness by David R. Hamilton
TED Talk by Elizabeth Dunn – Helping others makes us happier – but it matters how we do it
TED Talk by Nic Marks – The Happy Planet Index
#BeMoreUs https://bemoreus.org.uk/
LEARN
Live to Learn – speech by Tim Minchin
Maddie and Greg Youtube channel
LISTEN
Hiroaki Kawamichi et al. Soc Neurosci. 2015 Jan 2; 10(1): 16–26. Perceiving active listening activates the reward system and improves the impression of relevant experiences
The 5 Love Languages by Gary Chapman
MASSAGE
Field T et l. Int J Neurosci. 2005 Oct;115(10):1397-413. Cortisol decreases and serotonin and dopamine increase following massage therapy.
Field, T. Complement Ther Clin Pract. 2016 Aug;24:19-31. Massage therapy research review.
Turan N and Aşt TA. Gastroenterol Nurs. 2016 Jan-Feb;39(1):48-59. The Effect of Abdominal Massage on Constipation and Quality of Life.
Dorothea V. Atkins & David A. Eichler. Int J Ther Massage Bodywork. 2013; 6(1): 4-14. The Effects of Self-Massage on Osteoarthritis of the Knee: a Randomized, Controlled Trial
Carolien Wijker et al. Animals (Basel) 2019 Dec; 9(12): 1103. Process Evaluation of Animal-Assisted Therapy: Feasibility and Relevance of a Dog-Assisted Therapy Program in Adults with Autism Spectrum Disorder

MINDFULNESS

Psychologies Magazines and Life Labs

MISTAKES

Brilliant NLP : manage your emotions, think clearly and enjoy life by David Molden

MOTIVATION

Supercoach : 10 secrets to transform anyone's life by Michael Neill

MOVE

Pereira APS et al. J Geriatr Psychiatry Neurol. 2019 Jan;32(1):49-56. Music Therapy and Dance as Gait Rehabilitation in Patients With Parkinson Disease: A Review of Evidence.

Klimova B et al. Curr Alzheimer Res. 2017;14(12):1264-1269. Dancing as an Intervention Tool for People with Dementia: A Mini-Review Dancing and Dementia.

López-Ortiz C et al. Dev Med Child Neurol. 2019 Apr;61(4):393-398. Dance and rehabilitation in cerebral palsy: a systematic search and review.

TED Talk by Marily Oppezzo. Want to be more creative? Go for a walk

TED Talk by Nilofer Merchant. Got a meeting? Take a walk

In Praise Of Walking by Shane O'Mara

Kazuya Suwabe et al. PNAS October 9, 2018 115 (41) 10487-10492. Rapid stimulation of human dentate gyrus function with acute mild exercise

Haynes JT et al. Psychol Rep. 2019 Oct;122(5):1744-1754. Experimental Effects of Acute Exercise on Episodic Memory Function: Considerations for the Timing of Exercise.

MUSIC

Music as Medicine - Lyz Cooper, British Academy of Sound Therapy (BAST)

Allen K. et al. Normalization of hypertensive responses during ambulatory surgical stress by perioperative music. Psychosomatic Medicine, Vol. 63, May/June 2001, pp. 487-92.

Aldridge D., Gustoff D. and Neugebauer L. A pilot study of music therapy in the treatment of children with developmental delay. Complementary Therapies in Medicine, Vol. 3, October 1995, pp. 197-205.

Hanser S. B. and Thompson L. W. Effects of a music therapy strategy on depressed older adults. Stanford University School of Medicine. Journal of Gerontology, Vol. 49, November 1994, pp. 265-69.

Waldon E. G. The effects of group music therapy on mood states and cohesiveness in adult oncology patients. Journal of Music Therapy, Vol. 38, Fall 2001, pp. 212-38.

Burns D. S. The effect of the bonny method of guided imagery and music on the mood and life quality of cancer patients. Journal of Music Therapy, Vol. 38, Spring 2001, pp. 51-65.

Thoma, M. et al. The Effect of Music on the Human Stress Response. PLoS One. 2013; 8(8): e70156

NATURE

Berman M et al, Uni of Michigan 2008

White M.P. et al. Spending at least 120 minutes a week in nature is associated with good health and wellbeing. Scientific Reports, June 2019

Kelly P et al. Br J Sports Med. 2018 Jun;52(12):800-806. Walking on sunshine: scoping review of the evidence for walking and mental health.

PLAN

TED Talk by Daniel Levitin – How to stay calm when you know you'll be stressed

TED Talk by Daniel Goldstein – The battle between your present and future self.

PLAY

Stuff You Should Know Podcast

POSITIVITY

Change Your Life with NLP by Lindsey Agnes

TED Talk by Shawn Achor – The happy secret to better work

RELATIONSHIPS

Malcolm Gladwell. "Outliers" Little Brown 2008.

Quoidbach J et al. Psychol Sci. 2019 Aug;30(8):1111-1122. Happiness and Social Behavior.

TED Talk by Stefan Sagmeister – 7 rules for making more happiness

SELF-CARE

Benzo RP et al. Explore (NY). 2017 May – Jun;13(3):201-206. Compassion, Mindfulness, and the Happiness of Healthcare Workers.

Self-Compassion in difficult times – Kristin Neff

SENSES

Lundström JN et al. Front. Psychol., 05 September 2013. Maternal status regulates cortical responses to the body odor of newborns

SEX

Omgyes.com

SLOW DOWN

TED Talk by Lucy Cooke "Sloths! The strange life of the world's slowest mammal"

SOCIAL MEDIA

Negroni D, Gen Y Millennials, Launchbox 2017.

Vannucci A et al. J Affect Disord. 2017 Jan 1;207:163-166. Social media use and anxiety in emerging adults.

TED Talk by Sherry Turkle "Connected, but alone?"

STUFF

Stuffocation by James Wallman

TOUCH

Friedmann E et al. Pet ownership, social support, and one-year survival after acute myocardial infarction in the Cardiac Arrhythmia Suppression Trial (CAST) Am J Cardiol. 1995 Dec 15;76(17):1213-7.

Nagasawa M et al. Social evolution. Oxytocin-gaze positive loop and the coevolution of human-dog bonds. Science. 2015 Apr 17;348(6232):333-6

UNIQUENESS

The Four Tendencies by Gretchin Rubin

VALUES

Steve Pavlina https://www.stevepavlina.com/

TED Talk by Noeline Kirabo - 2 questions to uncover your passion - and turn it into a career

VISUAL

NLP Podcasts

WARM WORDS OF THE WORLD

Psychologies Magazines

WRITE

The morning papers by Julia Cameron

YOUR TRIBE

Poems by Susanna Michaelis

ZZZZ

Lyall, L et al. The Lancet. VOLUME 5, ISSUE 6, P507-514, JUNE 01, 2018

TED Talk by Matt Walker "Sleep is your superpower".

TED Talk by Russell Foster "Why do we sleep?"

Wagner U et al. Nature 2004 Jan 22;427(6972):352-5. Sleep inspires insight.

About the Author

A few facts about me that lead me to write this book:

- I'm a mum of two amazing girls who have taught me more about life and myself, than anything else!

- I'm a nearly qualified (delayed by covid-19) Neuro-linguistic Programming Practitioner and 'Ollie' Coach, helping children to cope with emotions.

- I'm an IAIM (International Association of Infant Massage) baby massage instructor, where I teach parents to massage and bond with their baby as well as holding group discussions about parenting highs and lows.

- I studied Zoology BSc with many elements of Biology and Psychology so have a passion for science of the human body and mind.

- I worked in Medical Science for 7 years, so have a love for research, interpretation and medical writing.

- I've been on the receiving end of many different forms of therapy from the age of 14 so I have tried & tested many methods myself. Researching and writing this book has also been an incredibly helpful and therapeutic journey.

- I am continuously learning, taking various courses around mental health, positive parenting methods, counselling skills and also continue to learn via TED Talks, Open University, FutureLearn, podcasts etc.

Printed in Great Britain
by Amazon